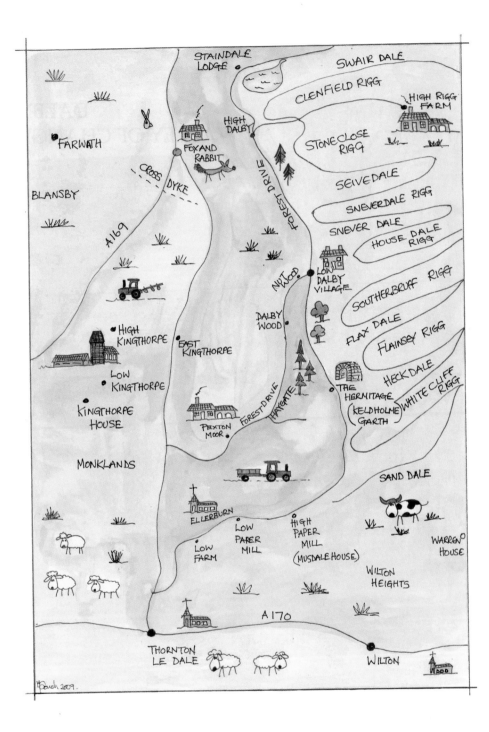

DALBY

VALLEY OF CHANGE

JOHN RUSHTON, MBE, BSc(Econ)

AND

BRIAN WALKER

 **Newby Books**

First published 1976
Second Edition 2009

© John Rushton & Brian Walker 2009
ISBN 978-1-872686-34-9

Newby Books, PO Box 40, Scarborough YO12 5TW
Telephone/Fax 01723 362713
www.newbybooks.co.uk

Front cover: Autumn at Haygate (Paul Hignett)
Back cover: Low Dalby (Peter Robson)
Frontispiece map by Mick Douch
Typeset in Book Antiqua by Brian Walker and Peter Robson

Printed by G H Smith & Son, Easingwold, York YO61 3AB
Telephone 01347 821329. Fax 01347 822576
www.ghsmith.com

FOREWORD

When John Rushton was asked to give the benefit of his considerable knowledge of local history to the Forest Education Project Group, a definitive history of the Dalby Valley was not envisaged. It appeared after an amazingly short space of time, delighting the group and reinforcing Mr Rushton's reputation as a local historian. His co-operation and guidance throughout the Project have been greatly appreciated.

Originally intended for use as background knowledge for teachers bringing visiting parties of school children into Dalby forest, the book is clearly of wider appeal and it is hoped that all visitors to the forest will enjoy their time spent here, all the more for having read these pages.

November 1976

FOREWORD TO THIS EDITION

In 1976 John Rushton's definitive history about Dalby Forest and the surrounding area was published in a hurry, with little proof reading and in very limited numbers. In the intervening years not only have requests for his book continued to arrive on the Forestry Commission's doorstep but also with the ending of the twentieth century another chapter in the history of Dalby Forest was waiting to be written. John Rushton kindly reviewed his original work and together we have made a number of corrections and amendments. Various tables have been transcribed or reworked, photographs added and a final chapter written to bring the work up to 2008, thirty-two years since the first edition.

Brian Walker
April 2009

A NOTE ON MEASUREMENTS, MONEY AND DATES

Land Area

Before the introduction of metric units based on the hectare, land area was usually measured in acres, roods and perches (poles). An acre is an area of 4840 square yards. There are 4 roods in 1 acre and 40 perches in 1 rood. Thus 5 2 31 means 5 acres 2 roods 31 perches. For comparison, an acre is equivalent to 0.405 hectare (a hectare is roughly $2^1/_2$ acres).

An oxgang, though not an exact measurement, was equivalent to about 15 acres.

Volume or Capacity

A bushel is a volume of 8 gallons or 36.37 litres. It is often used to measure quantities of grain. The weight of a bushel varies but, for example, a bushel of wheat weighs about 60lb (60 pounds or 27.2 kilograms). There are 8 bushels in 1 quarter.

Money

Decimalisation (division of a pound into 100 pence) was introduced in the UK in 1971. Prior to that time, the pound was divided into 240 pence (240d). There were 12 pence in 1 shilling (1s) and 20 shillings in 1 pound (£1). Thus £4 17s 5d (four pounds seventeen and five) was the old way of writing and saying (approximately) £4.87 (four pounds eighty-seven pence).

A mark was 13s 4d (two thirds of a pound).

Dates

In old documents and conversation, dates were often referred to by events in the Christian calendar, rather than by months and days. The following are those used in this book:-
Candlemas = February 2
Purification of the Blessed Virgin Mary = February 2
Annunciation of the Blessed Virgin Mary (Lady Day) = March 25
St William's Day = June 8
Midsummer's Day = June 24
Holy Rood Day = September 14
Michaelmas = September 29
Martinmas = November 11
St Thomas's Day = December 21
Nativity = December 25

CONTENTS

1

DALBY – VALLEY OF CHANGE

In a deep Yorkshire valley, four miles north-east of the old market town of Pickering, a tiny village called Low Dalby nestles beside open pastures and between dense forest plantations. Clear water is carried down the vale from the Staindale Beck and other tiny rivulets by a stream that is variously called the Dalby, Ellerburn and Thornton Beck. A quiet rural hamlet called Ellerburn stands downstream amidst more open ground where the valley widens. A mile further south where the beck enters the Vale of Pickering is the large and much visited pretty village of Thornton Dale.

Low Dalby is a Forestry Commission village newly created in the 20th century but has a handful of stone buildings that were there long before. High Dalby is a single private house further up the valley. The name Dalby is also given to a broad forest district nowadays. In the past, Dalby meant a small and ancient valley settlement and a bounded tract of small dales, hill ridges and moors, rising to five and seven hundred feet. Throughout much of history, the people at the hamlet settlement made their living from the resources within the boundary. Changes in climate and changes initiated by men and women altered the landscape many times and few areas have seen more dramatic changes in land-use.

Woodland was once the natural cover, even of the higher ground. For centuries, pre-historic people hunted its wildlife. With axes, fire and domestic animals they reduced the woodland area. Hilltop clearances, that must have been used by the people of nearby settlements in Romano-British times, gave way to a valley hamlet or village that the Vikings called Dalby. Under the Normans, during the 12th century, Dalby was given a specialised function within the broad Royal Forest of Pickering, while its neighbours went on farming their open arable fields, meadows and commons. Thereafter, its history was different to theirs.

The changing balance of arable cultivation, pastoral farming and wildlife hunting is the essence of much rural local history. Dalby was unusual in the primacy given within its bounds to maintenance of the deer. Yet, even in the Middle Ages, timber felling and minor extractive industries had their place while great sheep flocks were brought to pasture. Woodland destruction ultimately removed the favoured habitat of the deer, and scattered farmsteads were established. Later great tracts of ground were set aside as warrens for raising rabbits which survived into the time of Victorian high farming. Once the National prospects of farming marginal land had weakened, the Forestry Commission came to plant new woodland, once again giving Dalby a special role within a broad forest. The old forest had been managed to preserve the deer; the new is organised to produce timber.

STIRRINGS IN THE UPLAND FOREST

The first settlers moved through extensive high and low woodlands in north-east Yorkshire. Deep borings in the peat at Fen Bogs, five miles north of Dalby, suggest that the mixed oak forest of the high ground saw clearance on a modest scale in the Neolithic and early Bronze Ages. Even the small numbers of earlier Mesolithic people who relied chiefly on hunting may have made a modest change in woodlands near their temporary settlement. The Neolithic farmers who left a cluster of long barrows above Ebberston, east of Dalby, brought stock, chiefly cattle. Grassland was limited and the animals ate foliage as fodder. These people used fire and had polished stone axes for tree felling. Their small clearings saw modest cereal cultivation and the pasturing of cattle. After a few years, the yield of emmer wheat would decline and they would move to a new clearing. Tracks linked these temporary holdings which slowly affected a wide area. A deserted clearing would by natural regeneration regain birch and then oak, lime and elm trees. Yet, the drier weather may have hindered recovery and helped denude the limestone of its trees.

The middle and later Bronze Age saw more clearance. In warmer and drier times, a more numerous people, possessed of bronze axes and a greater number of sheep as well as cattle and pigs, made settlements on hill ridges. Dwarf animals held back regeneration on the poor pastures. Both oxen and pigs found food in forest undergrowth. Grasses, bracken, weeds and cereals increased. Sheep close-cropped low scrub and open ground. Marked increases in the scale of clearance came near late Bronze Age, Iron Age and Romano-British settlements. Some of these were where springs emerged from the lower limestone slopes where villages still stand, but others were on the table land of the higher ground, amid light upland soils. Use of the plough and some knowledge of manuring brought permanent cornfields into use near the villages. Pastoral farming based on small stock enclosures and perhaps ranches delineated by linear earthworks may have characterised the higher grounds. Iron sickles and Roman scythes allowed hay to be harvested. Sheep were more numerous. As heavier ploughs ate into lower land, pressure on the hill land was eased.

PREHISTORIC REMAINS

Only a few ancient burial mounds covering prehistoric graves have been found at Dalby but there are both clusters and isolated mounds on nearby high ground. Within Dalby were five mounds on Newclose Rigg and three on Adderstone Rigg, both parts of Dalby most remote from the valley. A cluster of seven mounds stood on the neighbouring Flainsey and White Cliff Riggs to the south-east. The westerly

Pexton Moor had four more. Such mounds were less likely to survive where later ploughing was deep and continuous. Dalby's high ground saw little late mediaeval ploughing, but the 1777 map seems to show five barrows on land later cleared for Riggs Farm. The whole area shows nothing comparable with the clusters of graves at Rustif Head near Lockton or at Thompson's Rigg further east. Yet, an area at the top of Flainsey Warren yielded large numbers of flint chippings and has been thought to be a place where tools were made.

Neolithic arrowhead found near Broadhead Farm by Paul Jenkins [Brian Walker, Forestry Commission]

7 cm

Isolated finds of arrowheads, stone tools and a bronze spearhead have come from the Dalby area. Recorded finds include:

Low Wood, Dalby	*SE 853876*	*Barbed & tanged flint arrowhead. Reported by T Hoggard.*
Pexton Moor	*SE 855857*	*Polished stone axe, possibly basalt, 3.75" by 2" by 0.8". Found by J Green.*
Monklands	*SE 836847*	*Polished flint axe, 3.75" by 1.5". Found by J Green. Four leaf shaped & five barbed & tanged arrowheads, several flint scrapers & knives. Found by J Gray. Others of both. Found by K Green.*
South of Crossdike	*SE 848875*	*Flint knife, reported by T Hoggard.*
High Dalby		*An "Arreton Down" type, Bronze Age spearhead*
Sneverdale Rigg	*SE 870887 & SE 868885*	*Hammer stone, green stone axe, and seven leaf shaped arrowheads, reported by T Hoggard.*

MEN OF IRON

Celtic people of the Iron Age made the greatest impact on high and low land alike. Their settlements have been found low by the Costa stream west of Pickering and at the bottom end of Thornton Dale as well as on areas of today's moorland. At Levisham Moor, two and a half miles north-west of Dalby, an important settlement worked small crop plots and included iron-workers. An impressive square earthwork still stands near the place and is clearly visible amidst the heather from Dundale. The Parisi people who came about 300 BC onto the limestone hills and the wolds are believed to have formed a stockmen's aristocracy surviving into Roman times. Small mounds in ditched squares mark some of their burials. Important graves contained their carts, sometimes called chariots.

Mr J Green, a gamekeeper to Thornton Dale Squire Hill, exposed an upright iron tyre, with remains of wood attached, while ferreting in 1911 at Pexton Moor, just west of the Dalby valley. The area has extensive earthworks. Dr J L Kirk made an excavation of what proved to be a burial mound containing the remains of the cart. The barrow was twenty feet across and four to five feet high standing within a rectangular ditched enclosure. It was re-excavated in 1935 by Miss A E Wesford. (SE 848856).

WITHIN THE ROMAN EMPIRE

The Romans came to north-east Yorkshire during the 1st century and absorbed the Iron Age settlements into a re-organised society. Finds of their time have come from Thornton Dale, Ebberston, Allerston, Pickering and a great many other local places. Some communities were geared to producing for the army and the new towns. Others continued pre-occupied with their own self-sufficiency. Sheep and cattle stocks probably increased. When the time came for the Legions to leave, a Romanised society continued and change was more gradual than was once believed. Some Romano-British farmsteads were on the limestone and greystone uplands. Annually, more evidence comes to light reinforcing older traditions of 'Roman' wells, houses, villas and settlements towards and beyond the northern fringe of the great open fields of the historical villages that would be taken over by the Anglians.

Within the bounds of Dalby, a silver coin of the Emperor Severus (193-211), a very worn Roman Bronze coin and a fragment of jet have been found at Hareborough Rigg (SE 868885) by Miss Laley, remote from any known settlement but at a familiar type of site. An upper beehive quern reported by Mr T Hoggard, 300 yards north-east of Rigg Farm, could be from the same period (SE 866890). A piece of grey Roman pottery – a rim of a flanged dish of 4th century Crambeck type – from an unknown site in 'Dalby Riggs', is in the Crosland collection. Nor is this all, for an old man from the village of Habton once told the archaeologist Mr Raymond

Hayes that he found a large quantity of pottery and three coins on Adderstone Rigg. He took them to York market where a man took liquid from a bottle to rub them and then gave him £1.00 a piece for them. His finds were made while ploughing for the Forestry Commission in the 1920's or 30's. Other Roman coins have come from Kirkdale Slack, south-west of Pexton Moor, and Romano-British pottery from near Blakey Farm and on Lockton Warren.

The place-names in the same parts of Dalby are unusual and probably have a bearing on Romano-British use of the riggs. The name 'borough' or 'brough' was often applied in old English to camps, earthworks and fortified places which the Anglians found when they settled. It is common near known Roman sites and along Roman roads. Two such names occur within Dalby, at Southerborough Rigg (now called Sutherbruff Rigg) and at Hareborough Rigg, just south of Seivedale and now called Sneverdale Rigg. An area to the north-west is called Cleufield though distant from Low Dalby and not known to have been cultivated during the late Middle Ages. A short trench joining Seivedale to Swairdale cuts off Cleufield Rigg from the rest of the high ground but is of unknown date. Lines on the 1777 map appear to continue to divide up the then high ground sheepwalks for no obvious purpose and to cut off the end of Southerborough Rigg. The old long-distance route near the limestone scarp passes through Dalby in the area, where finds have been made. A jet bead and a blue melon bead are reported by T Hoggard from west of the Cleufield entrenchment. (SE 870889).

ANGLIAN AND SCANDINAVIAN VILLAGES

The numbers of Anglian people expanded slowly from their first settlements in the Wolds to take over and develop old Celtic villages and perhaps found some new ones. Their eight-oxen ploughs brought heavier land into use but older modes of using land may for some time have continued in the high ground and valleys. Their townships of the limestone slopes were divided into great tracts of common arable field, common meadows on a much smaller scale and common pastures and wastes merging with the scrub and woodland now contracting before plough and hoof. Village settlements predominated outside the dales.

The name Thornton was given by the Anglians to the village at the dale-mouth. Yet around Thornton are places with Scandinavian names like Roxby, Liedthorpe and Farmanby. The Anglian settlement of the 6th and 7th centuries was followed by Viking movements of the 9th and 10th centuries. At Thornton, the village layout suggests that this resulted in new communities being grafted onto the old one. The small settlements in the long valley north of Thornton have similar names. Ellerburn meant 'a stream among the alder trees', giving its name to a small village where alders still grew in 1334. Dalby meant a dale farm, hamlet or village. Further

Low Dalby in the late 1960s
[From a slide by the late Jack Eaton, Forest Ranger]

north, within the bounds of modern Lockton, was the now lost settlement of Ketilthorpe, the farm or hamlet of a man called Ketil.

Fragments of early crosses make it clear that Ellerburn and Pickering had churches by Viking times. Those at Ellerburn are found re-used as masonry in various parts of the rebuilt church of Norman times. One crosshead has been attributed to c850 and another to the late 10th century. There is a fragment with carved figures and one cross shows a dragon. Pieces of early cablework and other stones bearing notches and spirals can be found in the walls, along with two 'hogback' grave-covers. It has also been thought that the chamfer edged altar stone was pre-Conquest. The church is dedicated to St Hilda, the 7th century abbess of the Anglian monastery at Whitby, and on either side of the chancel arch are roughly carved 'serpents', spirals known as St Hilda's snakes. She was credited with turning the snakes to stone in the characteristic fossils of the district. In Norman times, Ellerburn was within the broader Pickering Parish. The remoteness of its site, at a small village with tiny fields, make it seem likely that it was an early district church of the missionary period.

A MANOR AT THE COMING OF THE NORMANS

The first document mentioning Dalby is the Domesday Book of c1086. This tells us that before the Norman Conquest, in the time of King Edward the Confessor, Dalby was a manor with some 16 oxgangs of land. Its lord was Gospatric, who held several other local estates, including an 8 oxgang manor at Thornton Dale and a 3 oxgang manor at Ellerburn. No indication is given as to whether any of the Dalby oxgangs were held by tenants or whether the whole manor was held in demesne. If there were tenants, then four, or even eight, villein families would have formed the most numerous householders of a small village. If there were none, then Dalby may have been confined to a Hall and a few cottage houses. Oxgangs were shares of ploughed land, associated normally with shares in meadow, and with pasture and other rights in the unploughed wastes and woodlands. The narrow valley with its cold wet subsoils and timbered steep slopes offered limited possibilities for ploughing. The signs of rigg and furrow that often mark old ploughland are absent but later enclosure-names hint at an area once ploughed on the east side of the stream. Most of the west side of the valley floor was long used as meadow.

The Normans came to conquer England in 1066. A few years later, after risings in the northern shires, they devastated many villages in what has been called 'the harrying of the north'. Afterwards, survivors were concentrated in a few places to start the recovery. Broad estates were re-granted to Normans. King William himself kept many estates including Pickering where an early royal motte-and-bailey castle was built. He also took the deserted manor and 16 oxgangs of land at Dalby from Gospatric. While many of the king's properties were later granted out to others, Pickering and Dalby long remained with the Crown. The Manor of Dalby was heard of no more.

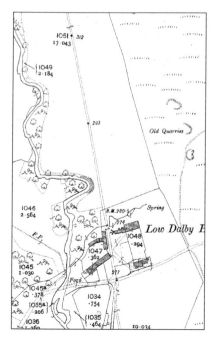

An extract from the 1910 edition of the OS 1:2500 map showing Low Dalby.
[Ordnance Survey]

2

DALBY AND THE ROYAL FOREST OF PICKERING

It was probably during 1106 that King Henry I on a visit to Pickering Castle declared that a wide district around it should become Royal Forest. To the Normans, a 'forest' was a hunting preserve rather than an area of continuous woodland. The 'foresters' appointed to keep it were primarily charged with maintaining the king's game. The Forest of Pickering extended from Sinnington, well west of the town, eastwards as far as the North Sea Coast. From the river Derwent southwards, it reached north into the High Moors to Lilla Cross and beyond Goathland. Within its boundaries, there were villages, ploughlands, meadows and treeless wastes as well as woods. This entire district was now subjected to special controls aimed at preserving the wild game for the king. He alone could chase, hunt or kill many animals and birds. Woodlands were protected too, but to provide cover, food and quiet for the game and most particularly for the deer. Dalby would become one of the places from which the Forest was managed.

Some local villages were fully active by 1086 but Dalby was not among them. Others were newly peopled during the 12th century as recovery slowly came. Though the Normans took the great estates from their former lords, they allowed some descendants to tenant smaller holdings. Gospatric's heirs were able to tenant a Crown Manor at nearby Allerston. By 1158, most of Dalby's neighbours once again had some residents. Local freeholders included Torfin at Allerston, William son of Norman of Ebberston, Engenaldus at Wilton, Richard son of Roger, Stephen Mauncevillain and Richard Rollevillain at Thornton, Walter son of William Bardolf and his sons Robert and Ralph at Farmanby along with brothers called Gamel and Gospatric at Roxby. Asketin Malecake was at Lockton, Ulfrik at Kingthorpe, Stephen son of Gamel and others at Pickering and both Thorold and Lucas were at Newton on Rawcliffe. No such men are recorded at Dalby.

Within the forest, some men were given estates to occupy as hereditary tenants, in return for guarding the forest or for training the king's hounds or hawks. One 'fee-forester' was settled at Kingthorpe, now a shrunken village, one and a half miles south-west of Dalby. Another fee-forester took one of the manors at Lockton and Levisham, two miles to the north-west. In 1160, 'Reynero' and 'Alano fratre Asketin' were the two fee-foresters. In 1165-6, it was their heirs William Boyes and Alan of Pickering who held office. The pair shared the 'service of keeping the Forest of Pickering' within the 'west ward'. This extended from the River Seven at Sinnington to the Skitter stream at Ruston near Wykeham. The foresters are not known to have had separate precincts within this broad tract. Alan's heirs were variously known as Malecake, Kingthorpe, Thornton and Pickering and they sometimes married members of the other forester's family.

DALBY LAUNDE – A HAVEN FOR THE DEER

The king's game was protected by the Law of the Forest. Its underlying principle was that hitherto ownerless animals belonged to the king. Hunting was viewed essentially as the pastime of kings and rights of forest hunting were jealously preserved. The king's 'beasts of the forest' which gave 'venison' were red deer, fallow deer, roe deer and wild boar. A wider range of beasts and fowl enjoyed similar protection but in rather few cases 'rights of chase' were granted by the king to other people and in rather more cases 'rights of warren'. Grants of rights of chase could include permission to hunt, and to exclude others from hunting fallow and roe deer, boar, wolf, hare, fox, marten, wild cat, badger, otter and squirrel. Offences in chases were punished at common law. No such rights were granted in Pickering Lythe West except in the Barony of Middleton, west of Pickering. Rights of warren were given to some local lords in charters that could specify hare, fox, badger, coney, pheasant, wildcat and partridge. Where not granted away, these too belonged to the Crown.

Red deer [Forestry Commission]

Two things ran counter to the new insistence on preservation of the game. Hunting and trapping had always provided a local supplement to the returns of farming. As the villages recovered, the pressure on the game increased. In a parallel development of the early and late 12th century, new Norman monasteries developed an increased use of the common wastelands. Village flocks were joined by large numbers of sheep managed from granges and high cotes acquired by the new communities of monks and nuns. In 1158, King Henry II gave the broad

'Marishes' below Pickering and Thornton to the Cistercian monks of Rievaulx Abbey. Two years later, Torfin of Allerston allowed them pasture rights for 500 sheep on moorland fringing Dalby, together with a sheepfold and half its muck. Alan Malecake gave Rosedale Priory nuns a Lockton farm with pasture for 200 sheep, 8 oxen, 2 horses, 10 cows, a bull, 10 sows and a boar, with their young up to one year old. He added a sheepfold, timber for mending it from Staindale, an acre at Ketilcroft and all his land at Ketilthorpe with rights for 200 more sheep in Lockton and Ketilthorpe pasture, at some time between c1180 and 1217. The nuns also had three houses at Farmanby. Alan also gave the Little Marish Priory nuns the right to take a horse-drawn cartload of wood for their ploughs every year from Staindale Wood. Meanwhile, Malton Priory gained a substantial grange at Kingthorpe. The Knight Templars gained manors at Lockton and Allerston. Norman and Osbert Bushell's manor of Ellerburn passed before 1148 to the Hospital of St Leonard at York but they let it to Alan of Kingthorpe. No monastery gained a foothold in Dalby itself.

At an unknown date, as pressure on the landscape and its wild life increased, two Crown estates were converted into 'hays', where the deer could run free and consume the herbage free from interruption. The sites chosen were not far from the fee-foresters' manors. The word 'hay' implies a hedge or fence and there may have been early boundary enclosures of some kind. Of the two havens, Blandsby Hay, two miles west of Dalby, was later converted into a 'park', with keeper's lodges and an encircling wall, within which the deer could more safely breed. Dalby remained a 'hay' but was also sometimes called a 'lawn' or 'launde'. It is not clear whether the two were co-extensive. Dalby Hay was sometimes spoken of separately from its 'vallies' and may not have encompassed the entire township area. Laundes were usually old clearings or natural open grasslands sheltered amidst woods. Blandsby and Dalby were both entirely in Crown hands. They were probably still empty of people. They had ample woodland cover and yet were sites within easy reach of the forester's manors and of Pickering Castle. By King John's time, their herbage had been set aside for the deer, because tenants of the king's demesnes at Pickering were then specifically excluded from pasturing their animals at Dalby although they had free run over much other ground.

PRIVILEGED TO HUNT

King Henry I enjoyed deer and boar hunting and there is little doubt that he, like many of his successors, took game in Pickering Forest. A Crown estate at Aislaby near Pickering was let to a tenant obliged to train a liam hound for use when the king came. King John was at Pickering Castle during February 1201, August 1208 and March 1210. During 1214, his huntsman Wyott took boars in parts of Pickering Forest where the king had hunted them. More often, the Keeper of Pickering Castle was ordered to supply game for the royal table wherever it might be and had to arrange long distance deliveries of venison. King John ordered Constable Peter Fitz

Herbert to assist the royal huntsman Edward who brought more hounds in 1214 to kill wild boars for salting down. Boars' heads taken by Wyott were soaked in wine. During July 1225, King Henry III sent huntsman Master Guy with John the Fool to take red deer for despatch to London. Again, during 1227, orders were sent for 20 hinds and 12 wild pigs and in 1231 for 50 hinds and 30 wild pigs.

Wild boar feeding on a fallow deer carcass.
Wild boar are once again roaming free in England
(although not in Dalby) [David White]

In time, a few lords, heads of great monasteries and some forest officers were allowed hunting privileges. King Henry I had ordered that hart, hind, wild boar and hawk should be reserved for the Crown in land that belonged to the Abbey of St Mary's, York between the Rivers Dove and Seven in Ryedale. This apparently left other deer to the abbot. It was perhaps as compensation for their loss that the monarch gave to St Mary's the tithe of venison in both flesh and hides, whoever took it, throughout the forests of Yorkshire. The king's larderers were to see that every tenth deer was delivered and received without hindrance. Even a tithe of dead deer was paid over and deliveries continued for centuries. In 1204, King John also gave the abbot the right to hunt fox and hare throughout his Yorkshire forests. In later days, the abbot sometimes came on deer hunts with the steward of Pickering forest and during King Henry VII's reign he received presents of deer that were not tithe.

Under the Charter of the Forest, archbishops and bishops, earls and barons journeying through a royal rorest to the King's Court were allowed to kill one or two deer, but only 'at the view' of the foresters. They were obliged to summon the forester by a blast on a horn. In 1259, the Master of the Order of the Knights

Templars took a stag as he passed over Blakey Moor in the company of the local forester Nicholas de Hastings and members of his household. His order had manors at Lockton and Allerston. Local manor lords could not hunt their own land without a specific grant or licence from the king or his justice, or in later days from the Master of the Game. When they were made, such grants did not include red deer or boar. In 1263, Stephen son of Peter had a licence to hunt hare, fox, badger and wildcat with his own hounds in Pickering Forest. Roger Ughtred of Ebberston and Scarborough gained similar privileges in c1253. Later grants were more permanent but were confined to hunting land within the 'acredykes' of certain townships. Sir Ralph Hastings would claim in 1334 that his ancestors had rights to hunt fox and hares within the acredykes of Allerston and Farmanby and to keep brachets or greyhounds. Where rights of warren existed, they were exclusive, allowing the owner to impound the nets, dogs and snares of others and to levy heavy fines on offenders. The owner could appoint his own 'forester' and there were such foresters locally at Cropton and Allerston.

OFFICERS OF THE FOREST

For most of its history, the forest was managed by local men appointed to part-time offices, and some full time deputies. Often their duties were merged with others concerning the castle, manor and honour of Pickering. The Steward of the Manor, the Constable of the Castle and the Master of the Forest was normally the same man. He was sometimes called the Master of the Game and the office eventually carried a general responsibility for both the 'venison' and the 'vert' or woodland cover. During the days when the royal castle was an important military post, the office was held by major royal officials who were not local nor always resident and who acted through deputies.

The 'foresters in fee' held land in return for carrying out their duties and the office passed from father to son. The holder carried a horn and enjoyed many perquisites. The two fee-foresters in the West Ward of the forest took 'attachments for pleas of the forest within their bayliwick'. In time, each had to appoint two or more full time under-foresters but sometimes called 'chief foresters'. Twelve other officials called 'regarders' were sworn in from among the substantial free-holders. Their task was to supervise boundaries and prevent encroachments within the whole forest. Four local 'agisters' controlled pasturing. Other keepers and foresters of 'park, hay and green' had their own 'walks' to supervise, or 'rides' if they were 'riding foresters'. In later days a 'ranger' was appointed to supervise the forest 'purlieus', areas near the forest which had once been under forest law. Near Pickering Forest, such areas included Ryedale, Haverfordlythe and Whitby Strand. The ranger brought stray deer back from them into the forest, and he sometimes acted as Deputy to the Master of the Game. Unlike Galtres Forest near York, Pickering does not seem to have had a permanent larderer, responsible for salting, storing and delivering game for the king.

An intimate connection between castle, manor, honour and forest management involved other local officials in some Forest responsibilities. The 'receiver' was a treasurer who collected money from bailiffs, reeves and others. Bailiffs were appointed by local manor lords. Reeves, often locally called 'graves' were appointed by their tenants. Both kept accounts of rents and other incomes received. Woodwards were appointed to supervise private woodlands but were sworn to keep the king's venison. They had power to attach and present offenders within their 'walks'. Any township with common within the forest could appoint four sworn 'bylawmen' to 'make good orders by the consent of the most part'. The reeve and four men from each township were required to attend some forest courts.

THE FOREST COURTS

The laws of the forest saw some development as time passed, drawing on local custom as well as on statutes and judicial decisions. The most important early statement of forest law was the Assize of the Forest of 1184 but it may have been a restatement in some respects of earlier practice. Important forest charters and ordinances were also issued in 1217, 1225, 1297, 1300, 1305 and 1306. Some were concerned with disafforestation. This was the subject of mediaeval political struggle. Substantial disafforestations were made by Kings Henry II, Henry III, John and Edward I but Pickering Forest remained intact. Despite the volume of national law, practices varied widely between different forests. It was later acknowledged that those who would be learned in the forest law ought carefully to study the assizes of the forests of Pickering, Lancaster and elsewhere, which were in the nature of year books to the forest laws.

Through the 12th and 13th centuries, the Justice of the Forests 'north of Trent' was the only person who could make judgements on the law of the forest. Later, the Earls of Lancaster received the right to appoint their own 'Justices of the Forest in Eyre', while an ordinance of 1306 allowed the justice to appoint a deputy and to take fines 'without tarrying for an Eyre'. The eyres were the high courts of the forest over which they presided. Four other officials called verderers, selected from the knightly class, were elected by the freeholders in the county court to preside over lower forest courts. Their symbol was the axe because much of their work was concerned with offences against the woodland. They had no salary and apparently few perquisites. Locally responsible at first to the Crown and later to the Duchy of Lancaster, they were obliged to view, receive and enrol all 'attachments' and 'presentments' of trespass of vert and venison. They kept records, attended all forest courts and were judges in those cases of vert, which in early days did not exceed the value of 2d, and later of 4d.

Forest eyres were courts called into being at the king's order by 'letters patent'. The sheriff received 'letters close' and notified the tenantry. Courts may once have been at seven year intervals but by the late 13th century were less regular. After the eyre of 1280, there was a prolonged gap lasting until the great eyre that began in 1334 and continued by adjournments till 1338. It dealt with an immense backlog of business. The justices heard and determined 'pleas of venison' and 'pleas of vert' separately. The record of both lawful and unlawful taking of vert and venison was reviewed. All free landowning tenants, the reeve and four men from each township, all past and present foresters, verderers, regarders and agisters or their heirs, and all those 'attached' since the last eyre were required to attend. Officers brought their records, known as 'rolls'. Those claiming liberties in the forest had to appear with their charters. The claims were discussed and either sanctioned, refused or curtailed. Township juries might attest the truth of statements but did not decide verdicts. Excuses for non-attendance called 'essoins' were considered first and absentees were rigorously fined. The long gaps between eyres meant that officers and offenders were often absent on bail, dead or untraceable.

There were several lower forest courts with different roles. 'Attachment courts' were held every 40 days, at which the verderers and foresters inspected attachments made by foresters and presentments of all offences of vert and venison. These were recorded on the verderer's rolls. At later dates, a court was held on St Thomas's Day at Pickering to receive presentments. At another court on St William's Day, oaths were taken at the same place from freemen and forest walkers. The Charter of the Forest required 'swanimote courts' to be held three times a year. At a swanimote, the attachment rolls were reviewed and either verdicts were given or cases were adjourned for the judgement of the eyre court. The verderer could 'amerce' for escapes, for pannage and for the taking of green and dry wood unless the damage was more than 4d. Swanimotes were held at Whitsuntide, Michaelmas and Martinmas. The agisters were required to attend the last two along with the verderers and foresters. The rolls recorded by the Clerk of Attachments were kept in the verderer's custody.

'Forest regards' were held every three years to inspect the woodlands for waste and to cover other matters. The sheriff appointed the regarders for this 'view of the forest' which could become a general survey of forest affairs. There was at least one in King John's time. At the regard of 1310, the sheriff summoned 12 regarders. Foresters had to be present and led the regarders to make the view. Any offences discovered went for trial by the verderers in the usual way. Other special inquiries were held from time to time and in later days special commissions largely superceded some of the earlier arrangements.

PUNISHING THE OFFENDER

Offenders could be 'attached' by their goods and chattels, by pledges and 'main prize' or 'by the body'. If taken by the body, it was for most offences necessary to find two pledges or give bail to appear at the next attachment court. For a second offence four pledges were necessary and for a third offence, eight had to be found but a fourth offence brought imprisonment. People from outside the forest were attached by the body for quite minor offences. Local people taking venison were always attached by the body. At the attachment court, an offender might 'mainprize' and could then be set at liberty until the eyre. The sheriff was normally ordered to arrest those who failed to appear at the eyre and after he had summoned them a number of times in county court, a sentence of outlawry could be made.

Justices in Eyre were bound to find 'remedy'. Early penalties for poaching deer were severe. It was within the 'king's pleasure' to order loss of life, eyes or genitals, in the early Norman years. The Charter of the Forest decreed that henceforth no man should lose his life or members for killing royal venison but King Richard I had threatened a return to the severe penalties of the past. By the Charter, a heavy fine had to be levied, and in default of payment imprisonment for a year and a day. On release, sureties for good behaviour were required or the offender could be banished from the realm. Offenders failing to appear at court saw their goods distrained. Fines for all offences were commonly related to the ability to pay and some were excused on the grounds of poverty. Many offenders had to find pledges for good behaviour. Fines for venison offences between 1334 and 1338 ranged from 1s to £2 and from 3s 4d to £1 for hare hunting. Later courts seem to have had the raising of income from fines and amercements as their main aim.

The available early records of offences are few but some are known. Torfin of Allerstone paid for forest trespass in 1176 and the men of Thornton were charged with taking wood in 1185-6. During autumn 1190, Geoffrey of Thornton, son of Alan the Forester of Kingthorpe was fined half a mark (one third of a pound) for bailing a trespasser who failed to appear. In 1230 and in 1241 Robert the Miller of Thornton took vert. With him in the latter year was Alan son of Geoffrey de Thornton and Alan son of Reginald de Farmanby. Roger Brun pastured cattle without licence. Judging by the numerous offences recorded when more details were available in later times, these may represent but a handful of the offences occurring among Dalby's neighbours. As time passed, more people and more domesticated animals increased the threat to forest beasts by poaching and disturbance. Burning, timber-felling and the close-cropping by sheep of seedlings among the herbage threatened their woodland cover. The number of forest officers was increased, perhaps resulting in a higher rate of arrest.

FINDING THE POACHER

Control of poaching operated by prevention as well as punishment. The 1184 Assize of the Forest ruled that no-one living within a forest should carry bows and arrows without permission. Even woodwards were restricted to carrying a small hatchet. 'Bow-bearer' was the title of a superior forest officer. How far the prohibition was maintained in later centuries is uncertain. Over time, many people with bows and arrows are mentioned in the records and later legislation would require the practice of archery as a military duty. The local one-arch bow of well-seasoned yew lasted until the 17th century and the arbalest or crossbow was already known in the Conqueror's time. When Will Watson was parson of Levisham, he used a 4lb crossbow for hunting and Sir Richard Cholmley's Blansby park-keepers found deer galled by long and cross bows. Arrows were carried in the belt or in a quiver, with the tips of the sheaf of 24 showing. Wands or stells for the shafts were made of birch, elder, hardbeam, oak and most usually of ash. Thought better short than long, they were feathered with goosewing or other feather to suit the wind. Fine bows were kept in canvas cases to avoid warping. As tall as the archer, they had strings of hemp or flax, and later silk. The range was from 100 to 400 yards. Best sheaf arrows had flat heads of steel and were not cheap. They were barbed for hunting in the late 13th century and in 1406 it was ordered that every arrow head or quarrel should have the mark of the maker. Hunting spears had small projecting wings at the base of the blade.

The ownership of large dogs, which could harm the deer, was severely restricted. The 1184 Assize forbade the keeping of greyhounds in a forest and King Henry II required that the feet of mastiffs in forests should be 'lawed', expedited' or 'lamed' so that they could do little hurt to the deer. By the Charter of the Forest, the regarders had to enquire about all dogs every third year. They made a charge of 3s for unexpedited dogs and were obliged to ensure that the three claws of a forefoot were cut off by the skin. The foot was placed on a one foot square, eight inch thick block of wood and the three claws struck off all at once with a mallet blow to a two inch chisel. Some religious houses were exempt and in the year 1326, 135 dogs were found unlawed in the whole of Pickering Forest. Owners were charged 3s for each dog, a payment called the 'hungeld', apparently almost equivalent to a dog licence, by that time. On one occasion, Chaplain John Valiant, who was leading greyhounds through the forest, was fined 6s 8d when the dogs escaped into Dalby Launde.

Throughout the year, anyone suspected of coming to hunt could be taken and imprisoned whether or not they had killed any deer. Possession of bows and arrows or greyhounds would raise suspicion and four situations were taken as conclusive evidence. 'Stable stand' was when anyone was seen, about to shoot deer, with long bow bent or crossbow at the ready, or standing by a tree with greyhounds in leash ready to let slip. 'Dogge draw' was when someone was seen with a dog drawing after a stricken beast. 'Backe beare' covered anyone found carrying away a slain deer. 'Bloody hand' was the term covering those found bearing blood in any suspicious way. The foresters could not only attach such suspects, but were bound to do so on pain of loss of office. Since local residents were sworn to keep the peace in the forest, if over the age of 12, they had a similar obligation. A forester or sworn man could call on nearby dwellers to follow the hue and cry to assist in pursuing and capturing any offenders. Those who failed to follow were liable to a fine. Parliament decreed in 1293 that no proceedings were to be taken against foresters, park-keepers and verderers who killed a poacher refusing arrest. It was once the custom in Pickering Forest to send a killed poacher's head back to Pickering Castle as evidence.

Special inquests were held by the under-bailiff, foresters and verderers with men from four neighbouring townships when a 'beast of the forest' was discovered dead or wounded. The verderer was bound to make enquiries about any injured deer and the finder had to give pledges for his appearance at the inquiry. The found deer had to be hung up by the forester or keeper till the inquest. An arrow in the animal was a perquisite of the verderer, and other 'engines' discovered were passed to him. Any offenders caught could be imprisoned until they found bail. Vert offenders were only bailed till the next attachment court but venison offenders were bailed till the next eyre. However, the attachment court could bail a vert offence to the eyre if it had been committed by an outsider or if it involved more then 4d in value. All deer killed or found dead were presented at court including those officially slain by people with a warrant or customary right. Many died of the murrain in 1286 and again after the wet summers of 1315 and 1316. The flesh of a deer found dead could be given to the poor and sick.

THE FORESTER OF DALBY

At some unknown date before the coronation of King Henry III, in 1216, a forester was appointed for Dalby. Up to that time, cattle strays found there had been a perquisite of the forest officer who found them. According to a jury in 1334 it was anciently the practice that whichever woodward or forester had found an escape in Dalby Launde had taken the profit of it, but afterwards a forester had been appointed with a fixed reward. The king ordered that if the forester that he or his heirs appointed found such an 'escape', before the fee-foresters (or their deputies), then it was to be presented at the attachment court and the king would get the profit. The fee-foresters had always been partly rewarded with privileges. As late as 1334, William de Percehay and Parnel de Kingthorpe, as fee-foresters, claimed 'escapes' in Blansby Hay throughout the year, and escapes in Dalby from Easter to Michaelmas. The escapes went to make up a yearly rent of £1 to the king. There were charges on each animal taken at a 1d a foot for the first or second time, provided they were not impounded by 'the King's Forester'. For a third offence the animal itself was forfeited. The jury denied this claim saying that 'after the inclosure of Blansby Park', the custom of escapes going as wages to the forester or woodward who found them had ceased.

The Dalby forester was also described as the 'keeper of the demesne meadows and dales of Dalby'. He was charged to preserve the king's game, the woods and the meadows, of which the last by the 14th century were yielding a hay crop, sometimes sent out of the dale. His payment was called a 'livery' and was made in a mixture of cereals called 'maslin' instead of money. The word 'meslin' later meant a mixture of wheat and rye grown together which kept free of mildew and produced a nutritious brown bread instead of the black, sour, long-lasting but heavy local rye bread. For the 20 weeks from 14th March to 1st August 1322, the Dalby forester was paid one quarter and 5½ bushels of maslin, valued at £1 5s 2½d. For the 26 weeks, from 31st January to 1st August, in another year, he was given 2 quarters and one bushel at 6s 5d the quarter, making 13s 7¼d. Prices varied from time to time. For the 25 weeks 30th January to 1st August 1326-7 he had 6 bushels of maslin at 5½d, and one quarter and 3 bushels at 3s 4d the quarter, making 7s 6½d. His allowance is said to have been a quarter every 12 weeks.

It seems likely that the forester and his family were the only permanent residents in the dale. Possibly, they will have occupied the old Manor site. In the later 14th century the foresters moved to a newer hermit's house further south but, for some time before, shepherds had been bringing demesne flocks to pasture the dale and consume the meadow hay. For that part of the year that they were here, they may at first have lived at the folds with their sheep. Since the main house at Low Dalby came to be called the Sheepcote, it is possible that they eventually replaced the forester there.

Poaching and the unauthorised removal of timber were probably checked by the presence of the forester. Few cases are reported from the valley and those were mainly committed by forest officials themselves. The fee-forester Edmund Hastings was said in 1336 to have kept 6 pigs in Dalby Launde, while another forester Hugh de Yeland of Ellerburn had a mare and 2 colts there 'under colour of his office'. His servant Adam, though unsworn, took pledges from people travelling through the forest and another servant Thomas Barry did so in the Hay. William, John and Hugh Yeland were all charged with poaching. The Dalby foresters themselves kept a few animals and may even have kept a small area of ploughland yielding the maslin. Henry Stainolf when forester in the Launde had six pigs. Another, Richard of Dalby, who took his name from the dale, had five pigs. John de Neville as Dalby Forester was charged 6d in 1338 for keeping unagisted pigs under colour of his office. Richard of Dalby appears to have made a career in forest administration. He had a servant Roger who was charged with taking pledges when not sworn and a son Richard accused of the same offence. He left the Dalby post to become a woodward at Cropton Castle for the Lords Wake. Subsequently, he appears at Brompton by Sawdon, where he probably served the demesne lords in the same office.

THE DUCHY OF LANCASTER

In 1267 King Henry III gave vast estates to his son Edmund, Earl of Lancaster. When Edmund's grandson was created a duke, these estates came to be known as the Duchy of Lancaster. The castle, manor and forest of Pickering, together with the king's demesnes at Dalby and land at Ellerburn, were a small part of the gift. Earl Edmund and his heirs were allowed to have their own justices of the forest whenever the king appointed them for his forests. They were allowed to keep the fines and ransoms arising from the eyre. After the revolt of Edmund's successor Earl Thomas in 1321 the estate would briefly revert to the Crown and when Henry Bolingbroke secured the throne in 1399 (as Henry IV) the Duchy became once again a Crown estate, but with separate identity and administration.

Under the Earls and Dukes of Lancaster, if not before, Dalby was used to provide several other resources besides pasture and covert for the deer. Local society had now recovered from the setbacks of early Norman times and pressure to exploit the landscape was much greater. In addition to the old borough market at Pickering, dating back at least to King John's time, a market and two annual fairs had been founded at Thornton Dale in 1281. By 1301, the village had two smiths and a carpenter and in 1332 a weaver, as well as a corn mill, fulling mill and common oven. Ellerburn had its own corn mill. The taking in of fresh 'assarts' was being allowed at the fringe of some of the local township's common fields.

At Dalby, stream-side meadows now supplied hay for the great Duchy sheep flocks which were brought sometimes to pasture the valleys and riggs. The earlier conversion of Blansby Hay into a walled park may have fostered this development. Dalby still saw the deer but was a little less secure as a sanctuary, the more it was used for other purposes. At some seasons the cattle, sheep and pigs of nearby tenants were allowed to pasture at Dalby in return for money payments. Timber was taken from the valley side woods while Dalby's high moor and its fringes provided alders, bracken, turf, peat, heather and either coal or more likely charcoal. At the lower end of the dale a hermit was allowed to settle.

When Earl Edmund died in 1297 there was meadow in Dalby Hay, at various places, worth £1 a year. The 'agistment' of Dalby and the adjoining dales was worth £3 a year. The 'turbary of Watmoor' yielded 5s in that year, 1s 3d in 1326-7, but nothing in 1325-6 when no licences were issued to extract turf from it. Another account of 1342 for the Dalby demesnes showed income of £1 10s 4d from the agistment, 2s 9d from escapes, 4s for stubble, turves and heather from the turbary of Watmoor 'sold in gross', and £1 6s 0d 'for one collyery in the demesne'. No alders had been sold, no wood felled for selling and 23 acres of meadow and a further 7 acres of meadow had yielded nothing. Their hay had been kept for sustaining the Lord's animals there. The reeve's account of 1351 showed similar returns but the turbary then brought 3s. There was nothing for 'coal' because of the defect of the works. Clearly demesne farming, and the letting of assets to provide income, were important features of Dalby life as well as the maintenance of the deer.

THE WAYS OF THE WILD BEASTS

Foresters and hunters built up a rich lore of the forest, expressed in a specialised language. Deer paths or 'racks' led between rest areas and feeding places where the deer browsed or grazed. At 'passes' they crossed streams and at 'smoots' went through hedge gaps. 'Entries' gave a way through fences or woods. Hunters studied the paths for footprints and traces.

Fallow deer [Forestry Commission]

From excrement, they could discover the place of the deer and 'their estate' or condition. Series of footprints were called a 'trace', while a single hart print was a 'slot'. 'Cleaves' were made by the two halves of a hoof and 'surcleaves' were the vestige marks of the other toes. Other footings were the 'vewe' of buck and fallow deer, the boar's 'treading', the hare's 'trace' and the fox's 'footing'. 'Fraying stock' showed where antlers rubbed against small trees, the 'scrapes' where the bark had been removed. Deer were 'in velvet' when their antlers were growing. After their prime they might shorten or 'go back'. The hunter would know his deer by 'view, feeding and fewmishing'. Slots, entries, ports, fraying and fewmits could tell him size and weight. Marks in the covert could reveal how the deer was in leg and side, or reveal the width of his horns. Young deer frayed saplings but an old deer would fray the velvet of his new grown horn on a higher tree. The good huntsman finished the day with a deer in good condition not a 'rascal'.

Hunters might 'rowse' a hart, 'dislodge' a buck, 'start' a hare, 'boult' a coney, or 'unkennel' a fox. At mating time, hart and buck were said 'to goeth to rut'. A roe went to his 'tourne', a boar to the 'brimme', hares and conies 'to the buck', a wolf to 'match' and a fox to 'clicketting'. Even the fats were distinguished, a deer giving 'sewet', while a hare gave 'grease', a hog gave 'saim' and roe supplied 'beviegrease'. Many other terms described characteristic features.

	Tail	Group	Ordure	Noise	At Rest	Season (time of grace)
Hart	tayle	herd	fewmits	bellows	harbours	Mid Summer Day to Holy Rood Day
Hind						Holy Rood Day to Candlemas
Buck		herd		groans	lodges	Mid Summer Day to Holy Rood Day
Doe	singe					Holyrood Day to Candlemas
Roebuck				bells	beds	Easter to Michaelmas
Roedoe		bevie				Michaelmas to Candlemas
Wild Boar	wreath	sounder or singular	lesses	screams		Nativity to Purification BVM
Hare	scut	husk, down or lease	crottels	beats	sits	Michaelmas to Mid Summer
Wolf	stearne	route		howls		Christmas to Annunciation BVM
Fox	bush or holy water spring	sculk or lease	syants	barks	kennels	Nativity to Annunciation BVM
Mottram		richesse				
Wildcat		clowder				
Coney	scut	lease or neast	taps	sits		

The large red deer herded in one-sex groups until the autumn rut, when a 'master-stag' gathered a herd of the smaller hinds, fighting off rivals or losing them to a new master. The five week rut was over by the end of October when hinds and calves moved to feeding grounds and the stags harboured in thick cover. Dropping their horns in March and April, they moved in herds to open heights to escape the flies of the covert as new horns grew covered in the tender velvet. Hinds dropped their calves in bracken or heather during late May and June, the white-spotted young staying hidden for a week with visits from the mother for suckling. After two months they could gallop and they would follow the mother for two years. Both sexes grew their long-haired coat in September shedding it in the spring. Herds fed in the evening and early morning on grass, heather shoots, moss, young leaves and tree shoots, but chewed the cud and slept through the day at the rest grounds.

The restless fallow deer were smaller than the red deer but larger than the roe. From the rut until the spring they formed smaller mixed groups. In the early year, does and last year's fawns frolicked together. Horns were dropped in May and re-grown by August. From the October rut, fawns born in May and June could run within a few hours. Bucks left the herd to secure territories for rut in mid-September and in October the does came to these traditional stands. Fawns ran with the doe till March when herds seeking new spring vegetation would move more widely and even enter the open fields. Emerging from the thickest available cover, fallow deer would wander, feeding at morning and dusk in open ground. In winter they kept moving, but on summer days would rest more in thick cover. Their paths remained in use for generations, and they adapted easily to life in parks.

The timid roe deer preferred the woodlands, coming out to feed at dusk and dawn but rarely far from cover. Except when driven, their small groups were rarely seen till mid-summer when they came to the glades. At the July and August rut, they ran in the ring. Afterwards bucks would retire to the high ground for the summer with second pairings during October. Thereafter family groups stayed together till May, when hinds drove their fawns away and dropped new fawns in thick cover. In two weeks, they would return with them to the bucks.

The beasts of the forest were further distinguished according to age, sex and development.

	1st Year	2nd Year	3rd Year	4th Year	5th Year	6th Year	7th Year
Red Deer Hart- male	calfe (vitulus cervi)	brocket, cervickno – bber (brocket- tus)	spaynard, spayard (spardus, or sorellus cervi)	staggard, (staggartus, or sourus cervi)	stag (staggus)	hart, hart of 1st head (cervus)	great hart, hart of great head
Hind- female	hindcalf (vitulus bisse)	hirsel, brocket's sister or hearse, (hirsula or ursula) hyrstel	hind (bissa or cerva)				
Fallow Deer Buck- male	fawne (juven- culus)	prickett, buck's prickett (pricket- tus)	sorrell (souelles)	soar, sore (sorus)	buck of 1st head, barebuck (damus)	great buck, buck of great head	
Doe- female	fawn (juven- cula)	tegg, pricket's sister, (tegga)	doe (dama)				
Roe Deer Buck- male (Capri- olus chevere- llus)	kid	gyrle	hemuse	roebuck of 1st head	fair roebuck		
Wild Boar (porcus sylves- tris)	pig of the hogge, Sounder	hogsteade	boar				
Hare	leveret	hare	Great hare				

In early times, 'feton' was a term to denote a red deer fawn. Raskell deer were those out of condition or too young to take. Venison (venacio) referred to all beasts of the forest.

Hart and buck were hunted when fat or 'in grease' from 24 June to 14 September. The hind and doe were taken from 11 November to 2 February. Summer venison was thought the greater delicacy. The greatest interest centred on the full grown hart. After its year as 'a hart of ten', it was described according to the increase of the head, whether 'croched, palmed or crowned'. The main horn was the 'beame'. The lowest antler was the brow antler, then the royal, the sub-royal and the top. In a buck, the order was bur, beame, braunch, adauncers, palme and spellers. According to some usage, rascal deer included all those with fewer than ten points. 'Warrentable' deer had ten or more. Hornless animals were appropriately termed 'humbled' or hummel deer.

PROTECTING THE DEER

Two seasons, winter and the fawning season, required special measures if deer stocks were to be maintained. Winter brought hardship to deer as to other animals. Fallow deer would herd up in holly, briar and heather, eating acorns, haws and sloes. Banks bare of snow, or sheltered corners of scrub, were vital for the roe deer. In hard winter, the foresters helped by spreading browsewood for them as a supplement to what was naturally available. This was usually cut in late autumn and stored for use. It had to be light enough for the deer to throw it with their horns, and oak twigs may have been mainly used. The giving of hay is not mentioned but people were paid 2d a day for cutting holly, ivy and oak bought for deer in the Pickering area in 1325-6.

Protection for the deer reached its maximum during the fence-month, the 31 days of the fawning season when the young deer were unable to run. Indeed this set the pattern for the forest year. It lasted from 15 days before Midsummer's Day until 15 days afterwards. The aim was to make sure that herds were replenished. On the first day, the forest officers made a 'drift' of the commons, impounding domestic animals found, for later recovery by their owners, at 1d a foot. Swine, sheep and goats found during the month were forfeited as 'escapes'. On the same day, at the Swanimote court, verderers, foresters, regarders, agisters and woodwards met to agree how 'watch and ward' should be kept during the month. No-one was to wander from the King's highway, or to drove cattle, sheep or swine to the pasture-grounds and wastes. Places frequented by the deer were to be particularly avoided. Pigs were kept in enclosures and cows could not be milked within 300 feet of woodland that gave covert. The Pickering ruling was that 'no man walk within the Forest during fence month unless a sworn man or have a sworn man in his company'. It was obligatory on any sworn man to present to the verderer those who did, and anyone walking suspiciously with dogs or bows, or seen to gather rushes and bent in the wastes and wood. It was a time to stay home.

Townships with a 'winderake', the right to pasture in forest demesne wastes belonging to the king, had brands for their stock. So too did those who were licensed to 'agist' animals in parts of the forest. These were branded on the drift day. Records of unagisted animals found at Dalby over several years of the early

14th century show the kind of stock then finding its way into the dale. In one fence month, the Launde held 4 pigs and 4 hogs of Nicholas, son of Roger of Lockton, 6 pigs found in an alder wood belonging to the vicar of Ellerburn, 6 pigs of the Rector of Thornton and 2 pigs and 2 hogs belonging to Peter Ulf. Another round-up brought 8 pigs, valued at 16s, belonging to Sir William Latimer of Thornton in the demesnes, 5 pigs of Alan the Reeve and 6 pigs of John Hart in the meadow. At various other times, they found 10 stirks, valued at £1 belonging to John of Roxby in the Hay, and 24 oxen in the meadow, worth 4s each, of forester William de Everley. Colts worth 1s 6d each were rounded up belonging to Geoffrey of Lythe, the Ellerburn vicar, Robert of the Cliff and two belonging to William, the late forester. Richard de Skelton had 5 horses in the hay and the under-forester impounded Richard de Wrelton's horse, worth 3s 4d. He restored John Prest of Ebberston to his horse on his agreeing to produce it at the eyre court. His surety was Richard de Dalby.

Sheep were found as well as pigs and horses. Most if not all belonged to owners of land in neighbouring villages. At different times, the drift brought in 27 belonging to Peter de Sartreye, 6 of William son of William, son of Ivetta de Ayton and 86 ewes of William Hastings, son of Lady Beatrice. She was one of the two wealthiest people at Farmanby near Thornton Dale. There were 40 wethers of the Preceptor of the Knights Hospitallers from Foulbridge near Snainton. Another 200 sheep were in the hands of Richard de Skelton and Matilda Prat, probably by inheritance.

Other drifts were made during the year. The Michaelmas drift could take place within the 20 days after and there was a drift on Holy Rood Day. Strays were not seized at the first drift, fifteen days before midsummer, if the owner was there to claim them, implying that a crowd of stock owners may have followed the officials. At Holy Rood Day, all animals found unbranded were taken in. Foresters and woodwards warned the villages of impending drifts. Animals were taken from the common waste to pounds at Pickering, where they were appraised by four freemen. The bailiff kept them for a year and a day, making three proclamations. In that time, owners could reclaim them and evidence of ownership from 'low borne witnesses' was acceptable. Fines of a penny a foot for first and second offences were paid. There was a charge for grass consumed and at later dates at least 4d a foot to the Constable. Charges rose over time. A 17th century document states that 'the like custom is for all the King Majesty's ageastments or demaines with the several braindes and if any be taken there couching or laying within the same and not branded, they are to be seized to His Majesty and fineable at 1s a foot'.

HUNTERS AND POACHERS

Scots raids adversely affected north-east Yorkshire in the early 14th century. In 1322 both Kingthorpe and Thornton Dale saw damage as a result of their attacks. In the preceding years, Earl Thomas of Lancaster had used his forest officials and tenants as a private army. Some 300 men in green jackets had been mustered to attack the king's favourite Piers Gaveston in Scarborough Castle in 1312 and many were taken further afield. An old legend tells that while a Pickering forest army marched to attack Scarborough, a Scarborough force attacked Pickering. One took the high road through Dalby and the other took the low road. Earl Thomas brought many new foresters to replace local officials, a source of much complaint. After Earl Thomas's execution in March 1322, William Latimer of Thornton seized Pickering Castle for the King. Among those charged with rebellion were William Page of Farmanby and the brothers William and Hugh Yelland of Ellerburn. King Edward II regained the Duchy estate, ordered 50 bucks and 12 hinds for his Christmas table from the Forest and build a new curtain wall at the Castle. He spent part of August 1323 there and hunted in his forest. John son of Ibote of Pickering gained 10s 'for following the King all day after a stag in Pickering Chase'. While the monarch was at Lockton, a bill of £5 was paid for large and small nets to take deer as the king passed. Beaters were probably employed to walk with the nets between them. The king's huntsman William was paid £1. The palfreyman who always followed the king received another. It was on 20 August, just before his departure that the king issued a charter to the hermit William of Dalby living at Flaxdale Foot. The monarch may well have hunted in the dale.

Many less official hunting expeditions were discovered but poachers were rarely reported in Dalby itself. Hugh and William Yelland of Ellerburn were known as persistent poachers though William at one time held office as a forester in the East Ward. In June 1309, William took a soar in Staindale Greens and carried it off to Allerston. On Sunday 28 June 1328, a William Yelland was said to have hunted a stag at South Little Dale in Dalby. It was later found dead and putrid in the cliff above the cow pasture there. Not far away, William son of Robert Todd of Kingthorpe, in December 1322, together with William Ashby, slew a hind near Newgate Foot and carried the carcass to Richard Campion's house at Farmanby. Geoffrey de Hull of Lockton was discovered poaching by the foresters but vanished on their appearance. John Scott was seen with bows and arrow but observing the forester did no harm and escaped.

A good impression of a poaching foray is given by Hugh Hasting's hunt on an October Wednesday during 1311. He led a party of twelve, including a woodward and the family's Allerston shepherd to Stockland and Hipperley. They took bows and arrows and laid on twelve gazehounds. They shot at a hart but missed it, when the foresters came upon them and captured 9 gazehounds, 2 bows, 6 arrows, a saddled horse, 2 costrels and a bag containing bread and herrings. In the same month, William son of Henry and Adam son of Ralph set a snare in the courtyard of John son of Alan of Thornton and caught a soar. John took the flesh and then sold the skin at York, using the proceeds to buy some fur for his overcoat.

There was all the difference in the world between a large scale official royal hunt with beaters and nets and the small expedition. Only rarely did the district see 'a stalk of foresters' and 'a blast of hunters' out together. Good runs are rare in any sort of hunting. The bringing to hand of a deer might be a day's work for a skilled hunter and his dogs. Back in the 12th century, Guy the 'venator' or hunter brought his trained 'lymer' hound to start the deer from the thicket, from Aislaby where he held 16 oxgangs of land for his services, but his son Richard commuted the service for a 40s rent. It may be significant that in 1301, there was an 'Alan the Hunter' living at Ellerburn, for such specialists were rare.

A 'harbourer' would put you onto an animal. 'Harbouring' meant finding the lair of the largest deer available. Fat stags tired more easily. Use of a limier hound, a keen-scented but mute animal, was the French way but the English method was to find the slot, track to a covert and cast around on the paths. The limier was swift and said to take its name from the stout thong by which it was held. The hounds had to be exercised, before the hunt began, to get them 'in wind'. Once the harbourer slotted the stag, he might move it, or would draw the covert with his hounds to get it on foot. Several varieties of hound might be used and over time breeds of staghounds, hart-hounds, buckhounds, harehounds and harriers were spoken of. 'Brach' were scenthounds, and the keeper of smallhounds a 'berceletter'. 'Berners' looked after the running hounds and 'ventrers' or 'fewterers', the greyhounds, which hunted by sight. The large strong mastiff could pull down a deer. Many a local hunt had only a couple of hounds available.

A chase could be prolonged. Hunting could be on foot or horse, in open or covert. It could run to nets or to a standstill. The suspicious red deer had good hearing, sight and smell and could detect a man up wind over a mile away. They avoided human tracks and were away at any unexpected sight, sound or smell, making up wind in file for their sanctuaries. The fallow, quick to move, were keen sighted and hard to stalk. They galloped and jumped well. The roe deer had even keener sight and hearing. The sure-footed red deer could walk, trot, canter or gallop and could leap fences up to six feet. Some, visible against heather, were easily lost in the green wood. Fresh hounds were as easily lost. The horn was used to call them together, when they broke away in a covert. The hounds would 'speak' at a find and the rider had to follow as best he could through undergrowth. Fresh deer might be roused in the course of a run. Initial success came by woodcraft, good houndwork and making good use of vantage points.

Hounds could tire and were sometimes used in relays. Horses needed rest more than the man. Deer would enter a stream to escape the hounds. Where they left it, the scent was weak, as water fell from their sides. The hunter might cast his hounds downstream while looking for clues in freshly splashed pebbles. Overhanging boughs might catch a scent. If the deer broke covert, the hounds would be laid on, and a racing run of one hour, two hours or more might follow.

The problem was to keep a good pace without running the horse to a standstill. Twenty miles could be covered in two hours and some local hunts started in one dale and ended in another far distant. Men could be used to turn back the deer but the rider had to keep up with his hounds to turn them. Deer would take a fence but avoid a highway. Scents stayed fresh on moist ground but if a deer was lost, a long cast might be needed in the direction he ought to have taken before a scent was picked up. With luck and skill, the hounds might pick out a line.

Deer stiffened when they lay after a run. If the hounds gained a view, they would get up to the exhausted deer, stood at bay. At a check, bloodhounds might be used. Even when shot, a deer could still rush up to 80 yards but the dogs would follow a blood trail. Once taken, the deer was laid on its back and drawn. Hunters carried daggers, or single edged knives in pouches, or slung from shoulder, belt or girdle, as well as cudgels to turn boughs. Part of the meat was given to the hounds. The brisket might be cut away and the head severed. The carcass was hurdled by tying its feet together so that it could be carried over one shoulder. Some would be hung for three or four days, others might be sewn up in hessian for despatch, once stiff. The entrails or 'humbles' went to make humble pie. A hind leg and half the rump made a 'haunch'.

Snares were also sometimes used to take deer. Cords fixed to stakes were placed in tracks with a bait to attract. Cart ropes and halters and 'engines called wires' were not unknown, and snaring nets. Buckstalls or deer hays with earth ramps and wattle fences could be used to take deer alive. In a large scale hunt, beaters might drive the deer towards such a palisaded or netted enclosure while men at 'trist' held hounds to intercept the wanderers. Some have wondered whether the funnel of linear earthworks at Scamridge Moor, Ebberston ever served such a purpose. Their date is unknown. An unexplained complex of earth works of star formation, but believed to be of three different periods, at the upper end of Blansby Park, may also have served some such purpose.

Hunting with falcons is little heard of in the records but certainly took place, until the advent of the fowling piece and the growth of the sport of shooting flying birds and small animals. The Normans fostered the art of teaching one bird to catch others. It is traditionally claimed that forest tenants guarded hawks for the early Norman kings at Killingnab Scar near Goathland, not far away from the 'Hunthouse' that was there by 1301. Sir John de Meaux owned aeries of falcons, merlins and sparrow hawks at Levisham and Thomas Wake owned sparrowhawks and merlins at Cropton in 1334, as allowed under the Forest Charter. By a statute of 1360-1 lost falcons had to be taken to the sheriff, who would proclaim them for two years. Imprisonment was the punishment for concealment.

Small arrows, made without a point, were called 'birdbolts', but birds were more often caught by using lime and nets, strings, baits, pitfalls, setting dogs, chaffnets, and even pipecalls, when the fowler whistled to beguile the birds. Partridges were illegally caught in the district with nets and limetwigs and a variety of bird traps set in the early 14th century. Local hair nooses for catching birds were called 'gilders' while snares were 'snicklers'. King Edward at Pickering in 1334 paid tithes of 531 waterfowl at 3s each making 13s 3d and on 157 heron and 5 egrets at 6d making 8s. Doves, on the other hand, were encouraged as a perquisite of manor lords. Farmanby had two dovecotes in the 15th century.

The wild long-legged razor-backed wild swine faded from local records in the 13th century, though once hunted on foot with a great spear. Wolves could be killed by anyone but survived in the Whitby district at least till 1394. Old wolfpits long remained as boundary marks at Greendyke near Ravenscar and north of Pickering. Foxes were at Levisham in the 13th century. As vermin, they could be hunted to earth and dug out, or otherwise killed - but not apparently in a forest. Foxhunting was sometimes used as a cover for hunting deer by those with rights of warren. Weasels were vermin too. Other animals hunted were distinguished as 'beasts of sweet or stinking flight'. In a judgement at Somerton in Somersetshire even hares were adjudged to be 'beasts of the Forest' and many offenders were charged with illegal hare-hunting in Pickering Forest, among them Geoffrey de Kingthorpe who 'caught hares to the terror of the deer'. They bred throughout the year and, renowned for their cunning, would double back or go through a flock of sheep to lose their scent. Coursing was usually done by sight.

PRESERVING THE WOODLAND

The woodland that gave cover for the deer was called 'vert'. Its preservation was vital for without vert the deer could not survive. Every plant bearing green leaf and offering cover was in some degree protected. The great wood, including ash and holly trees was 'over-vert' while 'nether-vert' embraced bushes, gorse and thorns. 'Special vert' enjoyed the greatest protection, normally considered to include trees bearing fruit such as pear and crab, hawthorn and black bush. Cutting these could bring heavier punishment. Royal demesne woods, whatever their character, including those at Dalby, were classed in their entirety as 'special vert'. They could only be touched with licence from a verderer. Local trespassers of special vert in King Edward III's time not only paid a heavy fine but forfeited their horse and cart.

Commoners did have some rights to wood within their townships but an important distinction was made by the 13th century between rights exercisable with or without the view or supervision of the foresters. By 1251, the men of the king's demesne of Pickering could gather dry sticks for fuel 'without view' but housebote, hedgebote, and ploughbote were 'at view'. Housebote could include green and dry wood for house building and repairs, taken at the 'livery of the foresters' in the king's woods. In other woods, haybote for hedging and fencing, walling for houses, and 'harz' for ploughs could be had by view of foresters. It was insisted that even the right to dry wood, which included wood they could knock down with their crooks, was 'at the will of the King' rather than a right. Tenants gave the foresters a halfpenny a year for every oxgang held, when 'the foresters made livery to them for making their hedges'. Hedgebote and haybote could be obtained if there was sufficient but not for giving away or sale. The insistence of the delivery by the forester was so that he chose which trees were used.

Even woodlands that belonged to the fee of other lords but which were within 'the regard of the Forest' had to be preserved to give covert and free movement to the deer. Ordinances of King Edward I's time laid down that wood for making houses and hedges could only be taken from private woods under a forester's supervision. In theory at least, the forester advised which felling might least hurt the deer. There was less concern if trees were felled away from great coverts. Manor lords commonly valued such woods at nothing in inquisitions. Freeholders had access to woods according to the fees from which they held land in a township to gather fuel or to obtain heavier timber from the forester.

Nonetheless, townships were regularly charged with wasting and despoiling woods in the early 14th century. Several woods close to Dalby were affected. The wasting resulted in the whole wood being seized into the overlord's hands until 'replevied' and a fine paid. In a typical charge, ten shillings damages were laid against Sir William Latimer, the townships of Thornton and Wilton and Richard Russell for wasting the woods of Ekedale, Flaxdale on the south, and Willerdale, all south of Dalby in 1338. The charges were apportioned at two shillings, one shilling and six pence, two shillings and one shilling Other woods affected were:

TOWNSHIP	WOODS WASTED		
Allerston	Crosscliff	Staindale	
Lockton	Crosscliff	Staindale	Horcum
Kingthorp	Westwood		
Thornton West, Farmanby and			
Roxby	Langatdale east (now Howldale)		
Thornton East	Kindlackside, Ekkedale, Flaxdale South,		
	Willer dale on the north		

A few woods within the bounds of the Forest were by charter 'outside the regard'. Other private woods were held with distinctive privileges. This was of some importance where iron was worked or charcoal burning carried on. Sir John de Meaux claimed hedgebote and housebote for himself, his men and tenants in Levisham woods. He took browsewood and dry wood for his smelting place there and made charcoal out of browsewood. Robert Short of Levisham burnt dry wood, probably for the same purpose in 1313-14. Private wood owners could also appoint a woodward charged to preserve the trees and undergrowth. Such officials had an accepted right to blown and fallen wood but not green wood. They carried an axe but not bows and arrows, to avoid suspicion of poaching. They could present vert and venison offences at attachment courts and took an oath. Among the local woodwards were those at Levisham, Allerston, Farmanby, Ebberston, Lockton, Thornton and the woodward of the Knights of St John. In 1347 it was said that the Ebberston woodward was chosen by two or three of the prominent inhabitants to guard the wood and common against strangers. Churches and monastic houses sometimes claimed privilege by charter. The Dean and Chapter of York claimed housebote, hedgebote, and underwood to enclose their curtilage and the township ditch at Ellerburn and Farmanby but their claim to ploughbote was denied.

THE DWINDLING WOODLANDS

Storm damage caused some loss of trees and the great gales of 1222 led to great forest surveys in the next year. Subsequently chief foresters had to make accounts of all trees felled for which they could not show good warrant. Great blown-down trees were called 'cablish' or 'rootfall' as against the smaller 'windfall'. Windfallen trees were often a perquisite of forest officers. Authorised felling was done from time to time, even at Dalby, and on some scale. An early 14th century Keeper of the Castle, Adam de Skelton sold 107 dry oaks from Dalby Dale. A Thornton Manor lord had 2 oaks from the demesne woods there. In the wider forest, Edmund Crauncester used 18 oaks to build a large house and Constable Hugh de Quilly used 110 oaks for castle fuel and repairs. Alders were sold from Dalby's damp Watmoor.

Felling was done during January-February, May-July and October-November to avoid the winter and the times when the sap was rising or falling. The woodmen used a simple socketed axe with a useable butt end. Carpenters were now present in several villages and must be assumed to have bought their supplies. The carpenter's axe was often T-shaped and could resemble a battle-axe. Indeed, there were several types. Felling axes were long and thin. A side-axe was the symbol of the verderer but the ordinary woodward had only a lopping axe or billhook, not a felling axe.

Charges of taking trees were more frequent than for taking game. Dalby in the early 14th century was not exempt. John White took the bark of a Dalby oak, which Henry Cockerell then cut down and carried away, probably to Ebberston. Thomas Sturmy took a green oak but died before he could be charged. John King, reeve to John de Drokenford took 5 oaks in Sandale, apparently as a gift of keeper Richard de Skelton. Peter de Neville, had a green oak in 'Ohwerdale' worth 2d, and his son Hugh was fined 2s. Henry Hockerell, while Dalby forester had vert worth 4s 4d. John de Shirburn, from a Wold edge village where timber was short, was charged

3s 4d for an oak, valued at 6d, that he removed from Staindale and took to Sherburn for housebuilding. Hugh de Neville was charged 2s 2d for vert in 'Chewerdale' and Thomas Sturmy paid 4s 4d for Dalby vert. Richard de Skelton paid 2s 6d for vert in Sandale and Eckdale.

Among others charged within a short span of years for removal of wood from Dalby 'without livery of the foresters or warrant' were:

Austin Crote	6 green oaks - value 6d - fine 6s
William son of Beatrice	6 " " " " " "
Peter Walnot	Small oak branches
Robert Tan of Ellerburn	8 green oaks - value 8d - fine 8s
Stut of Ellerburn	1 green oak
Austin the Reeve	1 green oak - value 1d - fine 1s
Stephen son of Alan	1 green oak

There was no provision for replanting. Woods recovered as much as nature and man would allow, by normal regeneration.

An old ash at Staindale. No truly ancient trees exist in Dalby Forest. [Brian Walker. Forestry Commission]

THE GREAT DUCHY SHEEP FLOCK

Two sheepmasters at Pickering had oversight of a large flock of sheep belonging to the Duchy of Lancaster. After the rebellion of Earl Thomas they briefly reverted to the Crown. It is not known when the flock was begun but it is clear that they were moved between high and low pastures and in some years were brought to Dalby. Here they wintered, pasturing the open ground of the valleys and riggs. Thornfolds were made to protect the sheep from the fox, shepherds stayed with the sheep and in time the main house in the dale came to be called the Sheepcote.

The flock was a source of substantial income from meat and wool, stored prior to sale in the woolhouse at Pickering Castle. Flocks were weeded out before shearing or as lambs and unpromising animals sold for what they would fetch. Even sheep that died had a value. Ewes were kept, probably under cover, unless it was very dry, from November to Easter to form the basis of the next year's flock. Sheep were sold as wethers, ewes, gimmers, hoggards, two-year-olds, lambs or rams. They were hardy, adapted to the severe weather of the hill grazings.

The Dalby meadow was the principal asset of the dale, though the acreage was never large. The Dalby forester looked after it until it was taken for sheep. Thomas the Forester in one year mowed the ground at a cost of 16s 5d and inclosed it at a cost of 6d. The inclosure may have been post and net but more natural material would probably be used. Other workers were brought in to assist. Cocklets of hay were set up to dry it, locally known as 'hipples' and the hay was raited by exposing it to the weather. Carts took it in some years to a distant sheepfold the location of which is not known but in others it may have been consumed at Dalby.

The following table shows some sample accounts

Expense	1325-6			1326-7		
	£	s	d	£	s	d
Mowing 47 acres of meadow in Dalby Dale and the Inclosure there, for the sheep, at 5d an acre	0	19	7	0	17	7½
Tedding, cocking, turning, stacking, spreading and remaking the hay, several times, by contract	0	11	0	0	10	0
Hire of carts to carry the hay to the sheepfold three to four mile and more, by contract	0	4	4	0	3	6
Five men, for 2 days, assisting the shepherd, to stack the hay in the sheepfold, being Autumn at 2d a day	0	1	8			

The acreage of hay and its value varied from year to year. In 1325-6, the hay cut for the sheep from 47 acres was valued at 1s 8d an acre, making £2 18s 4d. Mowing 40 acres and another 7 acres within an inclosure cost 17s 7½d in 1313-14. A further 7s 9d was spent on 'tedding', making it into hay and cocking it in the meadows. Then 4s 4d was paid for carrying it, stacking the hay in the granges and on the wages of those who led the carts. The total cost of £1 14s 0½d to be set against the income was reckoned high on account of rainy weather. Summer rains spoil hay and 'make hay while the sun shines' is an age-old expression. Rising costs of collection caused some concern to the Duchy officials. The keeper of the Accounts for 1325-6 reported that each acre cost '8d all but 5d' as against 5d an acre in earlier years. He said that this was because 'the meadows lay in a remote place, three miles from a village and in a valley within a wood'. In the next year mowing was done at 4½d an acre instead of 5d.

Quite apart from the use of the hay, the flock was sometimes brought to Dalby to pasture. When the four Duchy shepherds were there, they had a claim on the maslin. In one period, 29 September to 27 December, some five quarters and two bushels of maslin were issued at a quarter each to the 'park-keeper' and to 'four shepherds looking after the 'King's sheep' in Dalby'. One source also suggests that the stallions and mares often kept at Blansby Park were also brought to Dalby.

The Duchy accounts over a period of years give some picture of the management of the sheep flock.

THE STOCK RECORD	13-3-1322 to 8-11-1322	29-9-1325 to 30-9-1326	29-9-1326 to 29-9-1327	29-9-1327 to 27-12-?
Wethers in hand	1 489	1 230	1 194	1 119
Died before shearing	23	23	14 (pox)	21
Died after "	18	2	13	
Culls sold before "	41	38	61	
Hogs added	-	27	14	17
Delivered	1 407	1 194	1 119	1 115
Ewes received	101	107	98	118
Taken from rebels	23			
Died before		33	4	16
Culls sold before shearing & lambing		14	2	
Died after		1		
Gimmers added		39	26	14
Delivered	124	98	118	116
Hogs and Gimmers Received	43	31h* 48g*	55	31
Lambs added after last Michaelmas	61			
Hogs and Gimmers Died before shearing	10	16h 18g	22	
Died after shearing	3	2h 4g	2	
Sold	25			
Delivered	56	13h 26g	31	31
Lambs From Ewes	96	93	113	79
Died before tithing	19	27	12	5
Paid as tithe	8	7	10	
Died after tithing			2	
Weak culls sold	8		10	
Delivered	61	55	79	74

YIELD from the Flock	1322	1325/6	1326/7	1327-
Fleeces shorn from:				
Wethers	1,466		1,132	
Ewes	100		118	
Hogs/gimmers	53		33	
	---------		--------	
TOTAL	1,619	1,340	1,283	
Paid in tithe	161	134	128	
Delivered/Sold	1,458	1,206	1,155	
Weight of clean wool		8 sacks	6½ sacks	
Weight of refuse wool		12 stone	27 stone	
Locket wool from wethers	4½ stone		4½ stone	
Woolfells of dead sheep	34	90	40	
			(14w, 4e,	
			22h & g)	
Woolfells paid as tithe		9	4	
Woolfells sold		81	36	
Hides sold of dead sheep	22	9	15	21w, 16e
Lambskins from dead	19	31	14	5
Paid as tithe		3	1	4
Sold		37	28	31
Left				7

*h: hogs **g: gimmers

EXPENDITURE ON THE FLOCK IN 1325-6	£	s	d
20 gallons of sulphur at 4d each for sheep smear		6	8
5 stone of white fat at 2s each for sheep smear		10	0
7 stone 1lb of tallow at 1s 5d the stone		10	0
70 gallons of milk for 93 lambs		5	10
Earthenware vessels for collecting milk through the country			3
A woman collecting milk			4
Washing and shearing 1,329 sheep			3
10 men assisting the shepherd to wash and shear the sheep and to watch the washed sheep on the high moor at 1½d a day		1	3
4 men for 2 days rolling and repairing wool to lay in a pile at 3d a day		2	0
2 men for 2 days at 1½d a day, carrying wool to those rolling it and collecting locket wool			6
A tile bought to mark the sheep			3
Wages of a thatcher on the roof of the sheepfold for 10 days at 2½ a day		2	1
A man serving him, at 1½d a day		1	3
Yearly wages of four shepherds at 4s 6d each		18	0
Food and wages of a boy watching the ewes, 6 weeks while with lamb		2	0
Yearly wages of two stock-keepers		13	4
Hay from the 47 acres at Dalby, at 1s 8d the acre, used in the keep of 1,360 sheep	3	18	4
Carrying the hay, drawing it within the house and stacking it there		6	0
17 quarters, 2½ bushels, one peck of maslin at 6s 5d the quarter as liveries of four shepherds, each having a quarter every 12 weeks	5	11	3

INCOME 1325-6	£	s	d	
24 culled wethers sold at Martinmas, at 2s each.	2	8	0	
14 wethers and 14 ewes sold at Martinmas 1s 8d each	2	6	8	
7 sacks of clean wool at £7 the sack	49	0	0	
1 sack and 12 stone of refuse wool at £4 the sack and 2s 8d the stone	5	12	0	
5 stone of locket wool at 10d a stone		4	2	
81 woolfells sold in gross	2	0	0	
9 sheepskins and 28 lambskins sold in gross		1	6	½
The carcases of 50 sheep of which 49 died of the pox and were of little value		8	5	
Milk of 80 ewes		10	0	
Hay cut from 47 acres in Dalby meadows for the sheep at 1s 8d the acre	3	18	4	

THE AGISTMENT OF DALBY

Authorised pasturing for cattle, oxen, horses, sheep or pigs within the king's demesne lands, pastures, woods and wastes was called 'agistment'. It was allowed in some places by the time of King Henry II. Under the Duchy of Lancaster, Dalby was an agistment, regularly used, and forest residents could pay a weekly sum per head of stock for pasturing animals there, after the May or June haymaking until November. Other forest agistments were at Horcombe, Allantofts, Scalby, Wheeldale, Fullwood, High Moor, Scallamoor, Langdon and Blansby. Township reeves had to ensure that cattle entitled to agistment were marked with the appropriate brand. Early demand for access to some of these pastures may have been principally to build up plough animals. The four local knights who served as 'agisters' could limit pasturage in the interests of the deer. They collected the payments and kept annual accounts. The agistment of Dalby and the adjoining dales brought the duchy £3 in 1296, £7 1s 2d in 1309 and again in 1313-14, but between 13th March and 18th November 1322, a year of Scots raids yielded only 6s 10d. From September to September 1325-6, income was £1 7s 11d and in 1326-7 it was £3 18s 4d. In 1342 the income was only £1 10s 4d. The use of Dalby for agisting must have inhibited its role as a launde for the deer, particularly during the fence month, unless grazing was limited to certain areas.

The three annual swanimotes were timed to arrange the movement of stock in relation to the needs of the deer. At the court, 15 days before midsummer, the agisters met to arrange the fence month. The next court was 15 days before Michaelmas on Holy Rood Day when agistment of the woods began, as opposed to agistment of the herbage. The third court at Martinmas 15 days after Michaelmas, saw the agisters meet to receive the payment called 'pannage' for pasturing pigs. These pannage payments formed a separate item in the accounts, gathered for the whole forest. The total sum in 1322 was £1 17s 4½d. In 1325-6, it was £1 2s 6d 'due to the poverty of the tenants'. The right to agist pigs in the Crown demesne woods was confined to freemen and was limited to the 'mast season'. By the Charter of the Forest, payment was set at 2 pence a hog and 1 penny a pig. A halfpenny was paid for pigs under one year. Some paid in kind by giving the tenth pig. For the 60 day season, from Holy Rood Day till the Feast of St Martin in winter, the pigs ate acorns, oak and beech mast and autumn fall.

Pigs formed an important part of the mediaeval diet, possibly the most important source of meat. They kept their nutrient well after curing and took salt readily. They took three years to mature. To keep them through the winter, acorns and beech mast were collected. From spring to early autumn they needed grass and they were driven into the fields after harvest. Being hard to herd, they were not 'common-able' in some forests, but the men of the king's demesne at Pickering had common pasture for all cattle save goats and had mast for hogs, without paying pannage, in the 13th century, in some demesne woods, though not in Dalby and its vales. Drifts were taken at Dalby during the mast season, as they were in the fence month. In 1336 Edmund Hastings was charged for 6 pigs in the launde. Other discoveries at different times included 6 hogs of Roger the Long of Pickering, 5 pigs of Alan the Reeve, 8 pigs of William Latimer, 6 pigs of John Hert and 2 pigs in the hay worth 4 shillings of John son of Walter. One mast season Master William of Pickering was charged £3 15s for 50 of his pigs straying at Dalby.

DALBY AND THE CHURCH

Although Dalby never had a church or chapel, it contributed as tithes one tenth of any annual increase produced from the soil. The tithe of venison went to St Mary's Abbey, York. Some ordinary tithes of stock and crops seem to have been paid to the ancient church at Ellerburn. In Norman times, this was long a chapelry of the Parish of Pickering. The tithes of that parish including its chapelries had been given by King Henry I to the Archbishop of York, who passed them to the Dean of York. The dean's Rectory Manor at Pickering had tenants at Ellerburn, Kingthorpe, Wilton, Farmanby, Allerston and Ebberston. The dean claimed for himself, his men and his tenants, herbage in woods, pastures and commons, housebote, hedgebote, rods for ploughs, underwood for fences, browsewood and drywood, nuts and freedom from lawing of dogs, puture and pannage in the mast season, in these townships. Some of the deans and their tenants appear in the rolls for running unauthorised animals in Dalby.

The few Dalby residents probably used Ellerburn Church. This small chapel was rebuilt in the 12th century and saw some change in the next hundred years, the chancel arch being rebuilt and a lancet window placed in the south chancel wall. In 1231, the dean allowed a relative to have the church, together with its tithes of Farmanby, for life. In 1252 a joint vicarage was ordained for Ellerburn with Farmanby and Wilton. The vicar's income included tithe of the three cultures at Ellerburn, of the garths and of hemp and line. His income was stated as £6 13s 4d for the year 1291. The vicar also farmed a small glebe holding and his animals found their way into Dalby.

Thornton Dale church appears to have been founded later than that at Ellerburn, apparently on a manor linked with Thorpe Bassett. It existed during the 12th century, its parish including Thornton east and west of the beck, but with parts on the west intermingled with Farmanby and Roxby, which were in Ellerburn Parish. In 1322-3, the Thornton Dale rector, William de Bergh petitioned the king's council, claiming that he and his forebears had been accustomed to have common pasture for all manner of beasts, at all seasons of the year, as part of their glebe, in Dalby, Cleufield and Haverbergh, places adjoining Thornton and within the parish. Since Earl Thomas's death, they had been in the king's hands and he wished his rights restored. The judgement is not known but appears to claim part of Dalby for Thornton Parish. It could conceivably have arisen c1200-1225 when Gilbert son of Alan the Forester was parson of Thornton. In later years, some Dalby tithes were paid to Thornton Church.

A dale almost devoid of inhabitants, if sometimes alive with animals, made an ideal site for a man of religion to set up a hermitage. William of Dalby was a hermit of the early 14th century at the lower end of the valley. When King Edward was at Pickering on the 20 August 1323, he ordered the castle constable, John de Kilvington, to allow William de Dalby, the hermit of Dalby to have pasturage for another cow and its issue up to two years old, in addition to the pasture he already enjoyed for two cows and their issue. The rights were to remain as long as he remained a hermit. He must have been established under the Earl of Lancaster. The hermitage was near a small ford crossing the beck and not far from the boundary track up Flaxdale to Watmoor. Hermitages were commonly near routeways. To the north of his small plot was the stream from a spring running down to the beck. His pasture was called the 'vaccary' or cow pasture beneath the cliff in 1328. He must have died before 1351, since in that year, the house was occupied by the Dalby forester.

THE KING'S HIGHWAY

As a forest launde, Dalby could be expected to see slight traffic in the later Middle Ages. Yet, an ancient east-west route ran through the township. Indirect evidence suggests that this was a 'king's highway', one of the mediaeval class of roads along which the king's peace extended. Provisions governing their width were made in the 12th century and the clearance of undergrowth on either side was required during the 13th century. The long distance route of which it was a part has prehistoric burial mounds along its course. It is the most likely route to have been taken by those Hackness monks of the 11th century who moved to found a monastery at Lastingham. The earliest known north-east Yorkshire bridge, called 'Ormesbridge' was probably where it crossed the Derwent west of Hackness. Prior Reinfrid of Hackness died at the bridge.

From Hackness, the road ran up near Coombhill onto the old Low Moors. Staying close to the scarp edge overlooking Troutsdale, it traversed the Low Moors of Hutton Bushell, Wykeham, Brompton, Snainton, Ebberston, Allerston and Thornton before entering Dalby Moor. Here, it crossed Stoneclose Rigg by a course more direct than the later route made around 19th century inclosures. It ran down High Littledale to meet the north-south valley road somewhere near High Dalby. It is significant that Roman finds come from the area close by the road on Stone Close Rigg. Under different names, the road is mentioned in inclosure awards for the townships through which it passes as an ancient road, and is variously described as the highway leading to Hackness, Lockton or Kingthorpe. The Jinglebee cross stood where the road crossed a north-south route from Allerston to Lilla cross and Whitby. It was still there in 1619.

Within Dalby valley were roads of uncertain status on either side of the beck running north-south. Crossings were at Low Dalby, north of High Dalby and near the Hermitage in the 18th century. The Staindale valley diverted routes north of Dalby and does not appear to have been crossed by any route. Within Dalby valley, three branch routes left the west side road climbing up to join the king's highway called the Whitby Road, which ran from west Thornton over Kingthorpe Common towards Lockton. Another road from Thornton Dale's Whitbygate running over Thornton and Farmanby Commons and by the west of the Kirkdale fields to Ellerburn was a king's highway and that status could have extended once into the continuation of that route northwards into Dalby. Gamekeeper Brewster found the stone base of an ancient road to the moor in the wood at the top of Kirkdale. The roads on each side of the beck once carried on from Ellerburn to Dalby.

Of the westerly branch routes leaving the Dalby valley, the most northerly leading into Lockton township was a king's highway. Known as the Overscar Lane, it now continues to the Whitby-Pickering road. It may once have continued westwards to the mediaeval ford at Farwath. Within Dalby, the north-west corner of the township boundary projects northwards to include a length of the road along the edge of Dalby High Wood. A more southerly branch leads west from Dalby Beck to the present Fox and Rabbit Inn, continuing to Farwath as the Crossdale Road, and then onwards north of Blansby Park. Another road of undoubted anciency rose up the west Dalby valley slope north-westwards called the Lyddygate Way. Below Low Dalby, the Haygate rose south-westwards into Pexton Moor and on to Ellerburn and Thornton. East of Dalby the neighbouring township had old northerly routes called the Robin Hood's Bay road, the Staindale road and the Crosscliffe and Hackness roads. Thornton Dale's Outgang Way and Nabgate, south of Dalby, appear to have led into these, so avoiding passage into Dalby and the need to cross the lateral valleys of its landscape. The presence of the hermitage near a ford at the low end of Dalby may mark the route followed by travellers to the turf pits at Watmoor. In the 14th century, the ford was called Flaxdale Wath. This and other dales had paths linking Dalby valley to the moor.

It may be no accident that three westerly routes from Dalby led to the fee-foresters' villages of Lockton and Kingthorpe or to Thornton Dale by the Haygate. The latter could refer to Dalby Hay or to the use of the road for hay shipments to Kingthorpe, Ellerburn or Pickering. Movement of stock, sheep, pigs and horses for grazing along these routes and others from nearby villages is implicit in many records. People and vehicles were less often seen. Carts may early have been brought for moving turf and timber, but horseloads, sledgeloads and backburdens were probably more common. Turf-sledges long remained a local vehicle, their continued use producing deep rutted roads, which would be hollowed out by rain water. Wains with no fixed shafts but moved by ropes or with a single long pole, long ladder carts and two-wheeled light carts with long fixed shafts that served as handles are believed to have been in use. Horses and oxen were used with carts and long-carts but most things could be dealt with by pack animals.

A toll called 'cheminage' would be levied on people taking things such as timber or brushwood out of a royal forest and on the carriage of anything through a forest on horseback, carts or carriages, during fence month. It was not really aimed at residents but at those who came as merchants to buy and then sell elsewhere. The Charter of the Forest said that only foresters-in-fee could collect it, but they often acted through deputies, normally bow-bearing officers. The rate was then 2d a half year for carriage by carts, and ½d a half year for horses. Local backbearers were not allowed to sell the wood that they had rights to. The Scarborough burgesses, who formed one of the main local sources of demand for fuel, were freed from paying cheminage on timber, brushwood, turves, heather, bracken and other goods in the forest in fence month in 1253. For some centuries, they acquired turf and peat from Allerston, possibly drawing on Watmoor where pitholes were once a prominent feature, some dug along old dykes. Others were on Pexton Moor. Whitby Abbey annually delivered a quite different commodity through the forest:

some 2,000 herrings sent for onward carriage to York by c1200. This was paid to the Master and Brethren of the Hospital of St Peter or St Leonard, who early held a manor at Ellerburn. This was subsequently let to tenants. In 1248 the Whitby Abbot and Convent agreed to increase the payment to 3,000 good and seasonable herrings, 1,500 red and 1,500 white to be handed over at the Thornton crossroads on the morrow of St Andrew the Apostle.

EXTRACTIVE INDUSTRY

Apart from dry sticks, the most important local sources of fuel were obtained by surface cutting of turf and the quarrying of peat. A place where these were commonly cut was called a 'turbary'. Dalby's Watmoor, Walter Moor and Water Moor, as it is variously rendered, held an important turbary. In the same area, heather and bracken were gathered, probably for roofing. An entry in the Duchy accounts for 1325-6 states that no licence had been issued that year for digging turf or collecting heather at Watmoor. The same was true in 1322, but in 1342 the income from the Watmoor turbary was 4s, the fuel being 'sold in gross'. Turf was pared wet but peat was cut from the deeper bogs in spring at a working face.

In 1342 a useful sum was raised from what a 17th century transcript of a document describes as a colliery in the demesne at Dalby. This seems more likely to have been a reference to charcoal burning than coal graving. In 1351 the works had stopped. Charcoal was certainly made in nearby Levisham woods out of browsewood and dry sticks and about Staindale in mediaeval times. Iron was being worked at Levisham valleys by 1255 and a forge was active there in 1322. Near Staindale Lodge, just north of Dalby a slag heap has been found that could mark the site of a bloomery (SE 851 889). Iron-working consumed large quantities of wood as charcoal. Viewed as of great disturbance to the deer, it was controlled, but itinerant forges were allowed under licence. No document is known to suggest iron working at Dalby.

FOREST OFFICERS' PRIVILEGES AND THEIR ABUSE

Many forest officers were allowed specified perquisites. The clerk of the Justice's Court had a tree each year as part of his fee. Any bow-bearer had an annual spring-tree. A woodward could have blown windfall wood within his walk but was not to sell any of it green. In 1334, the fee-foresters claimed browsewood, after-pannage, drywood and nutgeld throughout their whole bailiwick within the Earl's demesne with some minor exceptions. They also claimed chips, bark and the treetops of any oaks and other trees given away or used by the Earl of Lancaster, though not of those that were sold. The jury decreed that the bark and strippings of housetrees were theirs by favour and not by right.

The fee-foresters' rights to saleable 'lop and top wood' could lead to abuse. They also had the boughs that they felled in winter for 'deer-fall', when the deer had consumed their foliage and in freeholder's woods could sell them. There was a temptation to cut more for their own use than for the deer. Fee-forester Sir William de Percehay was charged by the eyre jury with exceeding his right. He could cut from stems such browsewood as might be secured by his under-foresters' billhooks and hatchets, but could not sell great cranes of oak nor oak trees. They said that he cut off huge branches of oaks, severed from stems by the wind, and some that were hanging down to the ground. Some that were felled to the ground that he could not sever with his billhooks, he just took. He also dug up huge roots of oaks and carried away three cartloads of branches, stems and roots. He was restored to office after paying 13s 4d.

Fee-forester Thomas de Pickering and his wife Margaret attempted to enlarge their rights but were curtailed by the jury. In the Lockton demesne wood they claimed that none could lop branches or fell any tree without their consent, but that they could fell and give away at pleasure any tree, green or dry, and could give and sell dry trees without the view of the foresters. The jury agreed that, from ancient time, the fee foresters had felled green hue without leave for food for the deer but decreed that Thomas was not to fell green hue without leave of the foresters.

While the Levisham fee-forestership passed by marriage through a number of families, the Kingthorpe office came to the Hastings family. By the mid 13th century, they had settled at Roxby and Farmanby on the west side of Thornton le Dale. Nicholas de Hastings kept the chief house at Farmanby but granted his younger son Henry a capital house in Houndgate with Roxby land. The family also gained land that had belonged to Elred of Ellerburn. Hugh Hastings let an Ellerburn manor to William de Yelland but it returned to the family. When Petronilla de Kingthorpe's husband Roger de Manserge died before 1323, Hastings served as fee-forester on her behalf. When Ralph Hastings came of age, he had 9 oxgangs at Ellerburn, 32 oxgangs at Allerston and 26 oxgangs at Farmanby. A substantial owner and an important local figure, he seems to have gained the Kingthorpe estate by marriage and with it the hereditary fee-forestership. He also gained rights of free warren in 1329. At the 1334 eyre, he claimed, unsuccessfully, that he had common pasture for goats in the woods and moors of Allerston and Farmanby. Much disliked by the deer, goats 'tainted the pasture' and were not commonable in the forest. He was allowed claims to heather and bracken and to cut turves for his own use, but not to pasture goats.

Abuses by charging unlawful tolls or seizing animals were not unknown. Riding forester David de Wigan was much criticised for seizing people and cattle until payments were made to him. Sir Ralph Hastings' servants were said to exhort money from people who passed through the forest. Under-foresters tended to become virtual woodmongers. Sir Ralph Hastings' Farmanby woodward charged those without common rights ½d and 1d a week for dry wood. Fee-foresters attempted to convert customs into accepted rights. In the early days, it was customary to quarter under-foresters on tenants who were required in part or whole to maintain them for some days with food and drink. This claim to 'puture' included ale and bread for the man, oats for his horse and a loaf for his dog. The Forest Charter of 1217 required that none were to have such ales and oats except 'by view'. A 1306 statute forbade such claims against a man's will unless they were due 'of old right' and swanimotes were required to enquire into surcharges made by officers. Though foresters failed to establish these claims as rights, there is no doubt that they continued to be taken. Tenants paid strikes of oats at Lent for horse provender called 'foster oats'. Occupiers of houses at Lockton and Newton had to contribute hens between Christmas and Shrovetide. John Scot, a west ward forester, was said in 1336 to have charged the country with his living and that of his servants. Four under-foresters, David de Newton, Thomas de Newton, Henry Rippelay and Thomas de Dalby were fined for taking wool and sheaves 'by reason of their offices'. It became accepted later that the ranger had oats in the moor towns and some country towns for killing their foxes, at least until the passing of the statute for killing foxes and vermin. William Cut of Ellerburn as warrener of Castle Ings and keeper of the south part of the forest extorted 'board sheaves' in autumn, and wool.

The master forester, who could preside at local courts, was allowed to distribute some gifts of deer to others. He sometimes gave the fee-forester a deer for loan of his hounds. When a stealer of red or fallow deer was taken to Pickering Castle, he had to pay 6s 8d to the bailiff, constable or fee-forester and on committal the jailer had a further claim to 2s 6d. The offender also became due for 8 shillings weekly for his table, and 4 pence a week or 1 penny a night for his sleeping, but the date of these dues is not known. The 15th century fee-foresters, Sir Roger Hastings and his partner, claimed to be able to course twice yearly at the sufferance of the master forester. Hastings sought two stags and two bucks in summer and two hinds and two does in winter but this was disallowed. In another claim to 'ascadde' and a hyrsel each winter, and two shoulders and entrails of deer slain in Blansby, it was agreed that he had the left shoulder but that the right shoulder and entrails were at the disposal of the master forester. Nuts were an ancient prerogative of the fee-forester and could yield 4s 6d in nutgeld in 1325-6.

ASSARTING THE WASTE AND WOODS

Clearing fresh ground to make intakes was the greatest offence of all in a forest, for this destroyed the vert and thereby the venison without hope of regeneration. Inclosures from the waste with or without licence were called 'assarts'. Encroachments to build upon were called 'purprestures'. Uprooting trees to make plain or arable, or any change of covert to another purpose could only take place under licence. When it was allowed, by King Edward IV's time, the cleared ground could only be surrounded with a small ditch and a low hedge that it was possible for a deer to leap. Neither houses, swinecotes, barkeries nor even haystacks were welcome for they brought people and dogs to trouble the deer. Burning off of heather and bracken was also viewed as noxious.

Yet, in many townships, intakes were made under licence in the late 13th and early 14th centuries before the downswing in the economy eased the demand for land. Others were made without permission. On discovery, such a clearance was seized but could be redeemed, usually on payment of a fine. The size of this was originally at will but was eventually related to the size of the clearance. A sum was also compounded equivalent to the annual rents since the clearing was made. Men with private woods were also allowed to make enclosures around them as the extent of woodland narrowed. High ditches and hedges could be used to protect young trees from cattle until they became established.

Assarting within the king's woods was more serious. It could bring imprisonment at the first offence, until a fine was paid of double the usual amount. Offenders elsewhere were bailed up to the third offence. Dalby, as king's demesne, hence saw little fresh intaking. The hermitage may well have been the first. The dale kept its early mediaeval landscape of uninclosed grounds, with temporary fencing round part of the meadow. There was no village growth, or development of the scattered farmsteads, of the kind that characterised areas of late clearance in Farndale and Hartoft Dale, until the Middle Ages were over. Earl Thomas allowed Petronilla de Kingthorpe to assart and break up 20 acres of her waste for tillage, pasture and meadow at Sloethornhirn, Westlack and between Haugh and Whitemin and let her cut 7 acres of underwood in a hagg near Sheepgate and Stoneygate, provided she paid him 4s for the assart and one quarter from the proceeds of the sale of the wood. At Dalby, no such clearances are known.

3

DALBY – FROM FOREST TO FARMS

Major change came to Dalby when the Duchy of Lancaster began leasing its assets to others instead of managing them directly. A gap in the available records prevents us knowing exactly when this began. In July 1362 and again in January 1364, John of Gaunt, Earl of Lancaster complained that evildoers broke his parks and closes at Pickering, Thornton and Dalby. Similarly, in 1367, William Latimer, Lord of Thornton claimed that many men had broken down his closes there and stolen hares, conies, pheasants and partridges, trod down and consumed his corn and grass and assaulted his servants. After the Great Plague of 1348-9, the pressure of people on land had eased and the pestilence would recur again and again. Wages were rising and services harder to enforce. Deer were fewer and as the heads of the House of Lancaster ceased to visit their hunting grounds, there was a changed attitude to the forest.

The local villages did not collapse under the impact of plague. After two outbreaks, the Poll Tax of 1377 could still record 420 adult taxpayers at Pickering, 181 at Ebberston, 87 at Lockton, 77 at Allerston and Loft Marishes, 56 at Kingthorpe, 37 at Levisham, 30 at Wilton, 40 at Newton, 78 at Farmanby and 124 at Thornton Dale, Ellerburn and Calfscot. This last place is unidentified but could be in Thornton Marishes or at Dalby Hermitage. Such populations were adequate to sustain the common field farming. Yet the pressure for new intaking had eased, marginal land was less attractive and some land was lost to the plough and won for the sheep, whose wool was the rising cash crop. Direct monastic farming was giving way among Dalby's neighbours while tenant farmers played a greater role.

The Dalby agistment was the first property to be let but the date of the first known lease is 1485. Tenancies could have begun long before. The agistment was now called the 'herbage and pannage of the pastures of Dalby'. It was let with a house called the Sheepcote in the pasture and the right to fold sheep in the demesnes. Another agistment called Langdon, now Langdale, a few miles north-east of Dalby was let with it, under a rent payable at Easter and Michaelmas. The change seems to mark the end of direct Duchy sheep pasturing in the dale but could have been more apparent then real for the tenants were prominent local figures, the earliest either holding forest offices or related to those who did. Some are known to have been involved in sheep farming but it is not clear whether they pastured the dale themselves, put sub-tenants in or continued to collect annual agistment dues from others.

DATE	TENANT	OLD RENT			INCREASE			TERM OF YEARS
		£	s	d	£	s	d	
19.11.1485	John Eure (A William Eure was made Receiver in 1485)	13	14	4		10	0	
20.3.1494	John & Robert Buckton	11	0	0	1	0	0	7
2.7.1495	Sir John Pickering & Sir Richard Cholmely Esq (Sir John appointed Master of Woods & Game 1495)	12	0	0	1	6	8	14
1523	Roger Cholmeley	13	6	8		6	8	20
22.2.1542-3	Sir Richard Cholmeley	13	13	4				21
27.2.1560	Thomas Colby Esq	13	13	4				21
c1571-2	Maurice Barkley	13	13	4				31
11.1.1604	Ingram Frazer Esq Thomas Pudsey Esq (His wife Phillipa followed until 1624)	13	13	8				40
c1619	Mr Richard Dutton paid half rent of	13	13	4				
16.4.1624-5	William Darcy							Remainder
8.12.1633	Thomas Hassell of Stonegrave & William Ives (who occurs at Farmanby 1652-63)							
14.3.1633-4	James Brooks & Thomas Fairfax for use of Henry Robinson							
4.5.1641	Elizabeth Howard							15 At end of terms

18.7.1649	Alderman Henry Thompson of York & Richard Seaton				
9.2.1650-1	Ralph & Beatrice Hassell	10	13	4	
29.11.1666	Thomas Hassell & Mr Clement	10	14	0	21
		(Improve-			*at end of*
		ment £130)			11
2.5.1697	Mr Hassell & Mr Lassels	10	14	0	
		(With			
		Wheeldate			
		Rigg High			
		Moor)			
10.4.1705	Thomas Hassel & Mary Lassels	10	14	0	
		(Improved			7¾
		rent			*from*
		£162.6.0)			1728

Some leases made were at the reversion of existing terms. Some assigned freely to others. In Frazer's time, it was made clear that the rent of £13 13s 8d included £10 13s 8d for Dalby and £3 0s 0d for Langdon, but Langdon was inclosed and treated separately after 1614. Lessees had full power to sublet. By Queen Elizabeth's time most of the other local agistments had also been let off but one, Scallamore, had become a common.

THE FADING FOREST

It is possible that the clear leases of the agistment in the late 15th century formed one of a number of reforms introduced by a fresh forest administration appointed by King Henry VII. Tenants of the Hastings family or that family itself may have operated more informal arrangements earlier. Sir Leonard Hastings in 1455-6 still held Allerston, Farmanby, Ellerburn, Roxby and Kingthorpe together with a manor at Pickering. He had a private chaplain at Roxby or Kingthorpe and Sir Edmund Hastings sued the Pickering vicar for not finding a priest to say mass in his Kingthorpe chapel. It may also have been this family who buttressed Ellerburn chapel and paid for a chapel built on the south of its nave, 16½ft by 9 ft. The chapel has gone but its recessed arch remains. King Richard III appointed Edmund master forester in 1483, an office he continued to hold under King Henry VII till his death.

His son Roger was not appointed but retained his family office of fee-forester. With the appointment of members of the incoming Cholmeley and Eure families to the main offices, he was put under strong pressure to conform to new ways.

In 1489, it was reported that the game was much diminished by excessive hunting. The king wanted stocks replenished and ordered no hunts to be made for three years, an order renewed in 1494. Hunting was now a more sophisticated and fashionable affair. With richer clothes, even hunting costume had become stylised with stalking coats and hose. Skills in archery were part of the equipment of a gentleman. New general legislation had supplemented the old forest laws. In 1389-90 it had been laid down that no artificer, labourer, or layman with lands or tenements less than 40 shillings a year, and no priest or clerk with a living of less than £10 a year could keep greyhounds or dogs, or use ferrets, hays, nets, harepipes, cords or other engines to take deer, hare, conies or other 'gentleman's game'. Those who did could be imprisoned for a year and the ruling was applied in Pickering Forest. Hunting by night or with painted faces was proscribed in 1485-6. After 1498-9, those who kept nets called deer hayes or buckstalls were to pay £40 a month if they had no park. Hare killing was made subject to a forfeit of six shillings and eight pence in 1522-3. An Act of Parliament of 1493 forbade use of the crossbow without licence by any but lords or possessors of 200 marks in land.

Foresters continued to be appointed for Dalby well into the 16th century. Some also supervised Langdon, but at other times that dale had a separate forester. George Buckton of a noted Hackness family was appointed forester for Dalby and Langdon in 1487. William Buckton and his sons, relatives of the Dalby forester, were known as 'common hunters of the King's game'. Another of the family who shared in the agistment lease served for a time as deputy to the Lockton-Levisham fee-forester. John Buckton was charged with selling Langdale wood at Scarborough. In 1490-1 he and John Kemp, the steward's deputy-clerk, took five does in Blansby. He had hunts at Dalby and took another buck and does from Blansby in 1488-9. Richard Todd of Kingthorpe was another 'common destroyer of game' in 1498-9. The fee-forester Roger Cholmeley re-appointed Thomas Bellandine of Farmanby 'to keep the woods of Dalby' c1499. He was later said to have allowed the wood to be destroyed. Losses of deer were reported from time to time and John Keddy c1551 maimed deer with crossbows.

Dalby seems to have seen more hunting than before, some official and some not. A stag was taken at Longdale in Dalby on the 12th June 1493-4, a priest Richard Gryndston having half. A hind was killed for the steward at Stayndale on 12th July 1492-3. Roger Cholmeley and John Kemp hunted in 1498-9 when in August John Cut killed a Dalby stag. The next year a hind was killed in the dale and the year after two great harts. Steward Bryan Sandford slew brockets in the dale in June 1488-9 and November 1493-4. Timber was taken too. One steward was said to be so afraid of abbeys that he allowed them to destroy the deer and woods. On two occasions fee-forester Roger Hastings of Roxby had seven great oaks. Roger Chomeley gave Roger Hewetson two Dalby oaks and William Birdsall of Thornton two more.

Fragmentary forest court rolls show a glimpse of continuing Forest administration. A Thornton attachment court of June 1496-7 saw Dalby forester Thomas Bellandine present John Carter, Ralph Ffulstowe, John Lather, John Bracon and Robert Todd of Thornton and Edus Milburn for taking green timber. At the next Pickering court, Charles Kemp paid in 10d for agistment of pigs received from several people. At the Brompton attachment court of 1492-3, the bow-bearer and three foresters including Bellandine presented 12 people who cut green wood without leave and one who took five cartloads. At the Pickering turn court of 1492-3 it was reported that John Mayson had made affray on Bellandine. A court order of that year required the villages of Lockton, 'Kynthorp', Wilton, Farmanby and Ellerburn not to make any hogstyes in Dalby for the future, under the penalty for each default of 40d. Nor was anyone to put any hogs unringed into Dalby, with a penalty for each hog of 4d. It was reported that the village of Allerston had burnt the moors at Stonedale Granes and Netley Granes by command of Thomas Wildon, but against the Steward's command, to the damage of bucks and does.

Relationships between the new Master of the Game and the old fee-forester came almost to a state of open conflict. In March 1498-9, Sir Richard Cholmeley was given the principal forest offices, with his brother Sir Roger as Deputy and Sir Ralph Eure as Riding Forester. They were specifically commissioned to inquire into illegal pasturing, assarting and taking of wood and game. The dispute ended with the demise of Sir Roger Hastings. His son Francis c1519 sold both Roxby and Kingthorpe to the heir Sir Roger Cholmeley. After living at Kingthorpe for a time, Roger made Roxby a family seat. The third of the local line, another Sir Richard Cholmeley was also Master of the Forest. He was knighted when leading a force of local men at the battle of Musselburgh against the Scots. The 'big man' of the district, he was called 'the great black knight of the north'. He kept 50 to 60 men servants about his Roxby house, sometimes called a castle, which he rebuilt with dovecote and fishpond. They said that though 24 pieces of beef were put in the morning cookpot, there was sometimes no meat left when he came to take his meal. Cholmeley was reputed to be 'extra-ordinarily given to the love of women'. After the death of his first wife Margaret Conyers, he remarried Lord Scrope's widow 'a flaxen haired lady of uncommon beauty'.

In the long run the Cholmeleys proved no better than their predecessors at preserving the deer. Queen Elizabeth ordered a four year standstill on hunting, shooting and coursing of red or fallow deer, except the bucks and does to be delivered to her Council of the North and the fee deer of the master forester and his officers. Yet in 1591 the deer were reported greatly diminished. Red deer had been gradually confined in the East Ward and fallow deer in the West but the surveyor in 1619 reported that few red deer were left in the entire forest. For every one, he thought there might be 5000 sheep. The fallow deer were now meant to be confined to Blansby Park but shared it with 300 agisted cattle and wandered into adjoining fields. There was little covert for them left, except in Newton Dale, where they were disturbed by wood-stealers. Yet some deer were forced by the drought into Thornton's cornfields in 1615.

Local stewards still kept handbooks, partly copied out from those of their forebears, detailing forest custom, but now embellished with extracts from Manwood's Treatise on the Forest Laws, which itself drew on much continental material. As a result they became bookish and unrelated to local circumstances. The richer literature of forest and hunt now introduced distinctions between animals based on methods of hunting, their habits, new views of what was vermin and even biblical precedents. To 17th century steward, Gawine Pollard, beasts of the forest (silvestres) were the hart, hind, hare, boar and wolf, which 'haunted the woods by day and the plains by night'. Beasts of the chase (campestres) were the fox, mottram, buck, doe and roe, which were seen more in the fields and open hills by day. Beasts and fowl of warren were the hare, coney, pheasant and partridge, which could be hunted with large hawks. It is doubtful if they were ever ordinarily thought of in this way.

A petition to parliament in Oliver Cromwell's time was submitted by the men of Pickering Lythe who detailed the problems of living under an archaic Forest Law. They said that they could not keep any sheep within their own commons, nor get wood for house, plough and fence repairs without licence. The poor were unable to dig turf or cut brackens for fuel. The woodland had mostly been destroyed before the Civil War but there was still sufficient for the deer, most of which had been destroyed. The park was ample to hold the few deer that remained, yet it was still unlawful to walk in the fence month without a sworn man. They asked for Pickering Lythe to be disafforested. Blansby Park was disemparked and improved in 1641.

NEW INTAKES AND FARMSTEADS

The old hermitage seems to have housed the foresters until they ceased to be appointed. Yet, Robert Kiddy, forester in 1559 still received wages 'for keeping the meadow at Dalby, which was wont to make a mixture of grain at 8s per annum, as in preceding years'. This seems to mean that he was still paid in maslin and looked after the meadows further up the valley, near the Sheepcote, which had already become a tenant farm. By 1560, a Duchy official William Tusser had let the hermitage as a copyhold farm at a fixed rent.

```
                              RENT
c1560      Thomas Lacy        2s
           John Wilson        2s
c1580      Thomas Brockett    2s
1581-2     John Cant
1615-16    Thomas Dutton
1621       Christopher Tucker  2s    (late Thomas Dutton)
1651-7     Thomas Dutton      2s
1661       John Wilson        2s
c1728      Mr Henry Kirby     2s
```

The hermitage had begun as a cow pasture farm and probably continued as such while a forester's holding. Now it passed through the hands of a somewhat bewildering series of tenants.

A modest expansion was made by gentleman Thomas Brockett, described as paying 'the new rent of a parcel of land called Keldhouse Garth, near Dalby, within the Forest of Pickering, containing by estimation, one acre'. A report of 1586 said that he had 'inclosed four intakes in a place called Dawbie, containing by estimation 4 acres, being parcel of the Queen's Majesties demesnes' and had 'set up three haystacks in a certain place called Dawbie Privett and Southerbrough contrary to the Assize of the Forest'. He had also built houses. A query of 1619 asked the surveyor to enquire about 'the heremite close in Dalby (once) demised to Thomas Whitwell, forester there, and arrented at 2s per annum'. The answer recorded in 1621 was that John Carpenter had made a new lease of the copyhold of 'a close near Dalby called Keldhouse Garth or Heremite Close, of the yearly rent of 2s, containing about 6 acres, to Christopher Tucker which he holds in peace'. In some descriptions, it became plural as 'Keld House Garths'.

Intaking of fresh land had at last come to Dalby valley. The result was court disputes brought up by those who resisted the change. A renewed pressure on land was evident in many parts of the district. Population locally was rising again and continued to do so until curtailed by fresh outbreaks of epidemic disease. In many places, piecemeal inclosures of commons were vigorously resisted by others with common rights. Sir William Metham inclosing at Horcum in c1584 had 200 roods of his hedges burnt down in the night. The Duchy still applied restraint on unlicensed assarting. Immediately north of Dalby, in 1554-5 a house called a Hayhouse was built at Staindale. As a 'purpresture' it contravened the old forest rule that 'none should make purprestures or inclosures of waste ground or covert, build new houses, or set up haystacks, without licence'. It was ordered to be pulled down or the owner was to pay 40s. By 1580 Sir Richard Cholmeley had inclosed Stangate Bank and Crosdale site intakes and built a house on Haugh Rigg. Will Fletham had made 3 intakes in Stayndale and Hallesike, some 66 acres, with 2 haystacks and 2 houses.

Another newly inclosed Dalby farm appeared as a 'new rent' in 1581-2, paid by William Boyes, for 'improved lands in the King's waste in Pickering Forest, containing 40 acres, abutting on Dalby Beck, together with one acre taken from the waste in Lockton High Street'. He paid 13s 8d rent for the incroachments and still held them in King James I's time. Robert Trotter by 1580 had built a house in the side of Keldale.

At Keldhousegarth, John Cante seems to have built a new house apart from the hermitage site used by the foresters. Sir Richard Cholmeley's account of 1574-5 charged him for 'the new rent of Keldhouse Garth nigh Dalby containing one acre, and one house lately built on the waste, in the tenure of Thomas Brockett and John Hickes'. In 1586 Henry Cholmeley, made suit against William Metham 'a notorious trespasser' and Thomas Brockett about the herbage and pannage of Dalby and Langdon. Brockett faced another suit in the Duchy court concerning the herbage, pannage and pasture called Dalby and Dalby Rigg intakes in October 1615. His son Edward had been taken for baptism to Thornton Church on New Year's Day 1576.

A family called Dutton had an interest at different dates in Keld House Garth but also in the main Dalby holding, the Sheepcote, with the 'herbage and pannage and foldage'. They had been for some time in the district. A Richard Dutton was 'farmer' of Langdon in 1492-3 and forester there in 1516-17 and served on Crown juries. It was probably his younger son who, lacking an inheritance, was taken on by Sir Richard Cholmeley, to teach his daughter Katherine to play and sing. He did so with some effect. The lass was the apple of her father's eye. When it was arranged that she should marry Lord Lumley, a marriage settlement was drawn up and £1,000 paid over as part of her 'portion'. Come the wedding day, she fell on her knees before him crying that 'she might rather be carried to her grave' than marry the Lord for 'she could never love him'. She was in love with Dutton. The indulgent father agreed, saying 'rather than marry thee against thy will, I will lose my money'. Richard and Kate were allowed to wed and Cholmeley willed her £600 in cash.

The Duttons became virtual squires of Dalby through their connection with the Cholmeleys. Sir Richard had bought a Whitby estate in 1555 and a Richard Dutton of Whitby as a Roman Catholic is said to have been secretly married by a priest in a house-chapel at Ripley. Dutton took one Duchy lease in 1579. Cholmeley died in 1583 but his widow, known as 'Lady Scroope', lingered at Whitby where she, her daughter-in-law Margaret Cholmeley and her daughter Katherine Dutton appear as Catholic 'recusants' in 1590-2. Yet, in 1590 the Duttons were also listed as resident Catholics in Thornton parish and were keeping a resident tutor in Pickering parish. The High Commission jailed the two ladies in 1592-3 till they agreed to conform to the established church, at least nominally. In 1595 Mr Richard Dutton and his wife were again listed as Whitby recusants, but in 1600 the wife only was recusant and the husband merely recorded as a non-communicant.

Fathers and sons cannot always be easily distinguished in the record. Another Richard Dutton and his wife Dorothy were charged with failing to receive communion in Pickering parish at Easter 1591. Sir Henry Cholmeley had moved from Whitby back to Roxby on his mother's death in 1598, where he left a reputation for high living, fleet hounds and horses, and having too many servants. His son and heir, born there in 1580, was another Sir Richard and himself would father Sir Hugh Cholmeley the Civil War defender of Scarborough Castle. The younger Duttons formed part of the estate staff as well as farming in Dalby. In 1607, Frances wife of Richard Dutton was charged with being a recusant at Dalby. In 1610-11 Richard paid half the rent for the herbage and pannage of Dalby. Robert Hunter, lord of a Thornton Manor brought a suit against Richard, his son Thomas, and James Winchecombe concerning their title to Keldehousegarth, Dalby or Dalby Riggs and Langdon in 1608, at which date Richard also had a lease of Blansby Park. About 1611, Richard was said to have taken down and carried away an ancient fair barn at Dalby of five bays. This may well have been the old Sheepcote itself.

The lawcourts had replaced the sword as a way of pursuing feuds and settling disputes. It was a litigious time. Henry Cholmeley as administrator of Richard Dutton's will, proceeded against Thomas Dutton, John Winchcombe, Will Preston and others for intrusion on ground called Dalby Hagg as well as for wrongful possession of houses and lands and for wasting and spoiling woods. He was also fee-forester in the west ward and tried to establish the legality of his claim to hens from houses supplied with firewood. The Cholmeleys themselves were now reducing their interests in the district. Roxby was sold in 1612 and Kingthorpe c1641. The widowed Mrs Dutton seems to have lived at Keldhousegarth in 1651 and Thomas Dutton described as 'gentleman' was there still in 1657. Three years later, it had passed to John Wilson. Nothing is known of him though a Thomas Wilson was Thornton Dale schoolmaster and Ellerburn church minister in 1690.

FROM TIMBER TO COPPICE

The Duchy surveyor of 1619 said 'there is little timber left in the Forest. It hath been taken and felled long since'. Wood had continued to be felled officially and unofficially. Sir Reynold Bray had reported waste of 94 oaks at Dalby Brow, Forester Tom Bellandine was said to have sold and given away yearly wood to the value of 5 marks. During Elizabeth's reign, the Earl of Westmorland, related by marriage to the Cholmeleys and then Master of the Forest and Game had given Cuthbert Chilton 7 oaks, each worth 8d, from the queen's woods in Dalby. On an official order from the Surveyor of Woods, Will Metham carried away 6 oak trees for repairing the nether mill at Pickering. One surveyor reported that 'in the haggs of Dalby, there is 40 timber trees of oak'. The great trees had largely gone. Haggs were coppices in local speech.

Awareness of national loss of timber supplies had come in the 15th century. Acts of parliament of 1543-4 and 1570-1 had required encoppicement in royal forests to replenish stocks, at least of small wood, and ordered twelve standells to be left on each acre in a copse felled after 24 years. The old forest laws had done something for conservation of existing trees but little to help regeneration other than by natural growth. Now nature was to be assisted: fences were required after cutting, for stated terms of years, to keep deer and cattle out so that seedlings might grow from seeds put out by parent standards or surviving large trees. Woodland management became an art and in a well managed wood, oak scrubs, 40 year old saplings, coppice wood and 200 year old oaks could be found.

Woods were now cultivated purposely to produce a crop of small wood every few years rather than single trunks of great age. Ideally coppicement of the lower layer of oak and hazel and other deciduous trees was combined with the retention of 'standards', fully grown trees to produce large timber. The first coppices just grew but improved methods crept in to 'spring' felled trees a few inches above the ground. The method of thinning was crucial. Young trees cut over close to the ground would in the next season send up shoots from the 'stool or stump' and from surface roots. Stubs of old trees this way quickly gave a second crop of wood. Indeed crops of small wood could be produced every few years. Cutting off the main stem of a sapling caused it to 'coppice' or sprout from side buds that would not otherwise have grown. The bark of stools was left as complete as possible and the ground was cleared of fallen timber and topwood. Fences were made up before the young shoots appeared, to keep stock out of the 'young springs' though sometimes thinning was done by controlled browsing. 'Looking' meant weeding which took out useless underwood and cross-growing timberlings to give air and room to others. 'Encoppicing' was assisted natural regeneration.

First thinnings came as soon as there was an undergrowth large enough to produce stakes, perhaps after ten years, and a second when the poles were long enough for rails, perhaps after 20 years, and thereafter decade by decade. Oak copse would be cut when 15-30 years old, when stems might be of six inches diameter. Other woods might stand cutting at five to seven year intervals, ideally on a sort of rotation. Hazel for hurdles was reckoned to need 9 to 12 years and ash for poles 15 years growth. Once a coppice was established it would be leased for a term of years, but with restrictive clauses on the use of wood.

Humphrey Farrer made a survey of woods belonging to the Crown in Pickering Lythe in 1587. In Elizabeth's reign two of the Dalby Haggs were let off while the others were kept in hand.

DATE	TENANT	HAGGS	ANNUAL RENT	TERM OF YEARS
Time of Elizabeth	Robert Barniston	Dalby Haggs (24 acres)	1 0 0	21
1594-5	Robert Younglove	Dalby Haggs	1 0 0	
1598	Thomas Dutton	" "	1 0 0	
c1598	Henry Cholmeley	" "	1 0 0	21
1626	William Popell	Low Springe Hagg & Risestye alias Haygate		31
ND	Thomas Pudsey	Dalby Haggs	1 0 0	
1628	William Darcy	" "		remainder
1633	Thomas Hassell & William Ives	" "		remainder
1699	Sir Humphrey Edwin	" "	1 0 0	11 from 1717

Encoppicement was not initially a great success at Dalby due to the shortage of great trees and to overcropping. The haggs kept in hand were in 1618 described as '15 acres in Swinegate Hagg, 20 acres in Lower Hagg and 18 acres in Spring Hagg, which at 6d a tree, are worth together £4 5s. The other three of the Prince's Haggs at Dalby, being of late cut in three or four years a hagg, making the last cut wood at the seven years end are so young that it is spoilt thereby'. The surveyor thought that Littlegate, Haygate and Low Haggs, duly preserved, could yield good profit, as wood was getting scarce in the forest. The herbage and pannage of the haggs was let off on lease but the woods belonged to 'His Highness'. Another report described Upper Dalby Hagg as 'of 12 acres, the wood of 16 years growth but destroyed and wasted'. Nether Dalby Hagg was some '28 acres, of 11 years growth, valued at 5s an acre and fit to be sold'. Values of wood at Dalby were low since it was hard to come at in the crags and dales and there was a distance to carry it.

Old Earl Thomas back in the 14th century had taken great oaks for fuel but those days were over. Housebote timber was now scanty and many of the district's cruck framed houses dating back to the 17th century and beyond contain timbers that have been re-used again and again. Trees were now carried long distances from the remote places where good oaks survived. Sir Richard Cholmeley used 120 oaks, sawn and framed at Goathland by wright George Barnard, to make his Roxby gallery, together with 14 wainload of stone and two of slate purloined from Pickering Castle. More ordinary houses still had the framework of three or more pairs of oak 'crucks' or 'forks' joined at the apex to form an inverted V, by a saddle bearing a great ridgebeam, and the V converted to an A by another beam further down. Extra bays, often some 16ft apart, could be added. Timber shortage during the late 17th and 18th centuries hindered new building but many were rebuilt, a few with the framework raised up. Others were given new internal upper floors and inside partitions. Many gained claddings of stone to replace old timber wallplates. Haver straw and many other materials were sewn to the riven oak spars and lats between the wallplates or walls and the ridge tree to form the thatch roof. In Georgian times, oak was gradually laid aside by the house-carpenter except for door and window lintels and internal wallplates.

Yet small wood long remained the most generally available raw material for making durable goods. There was a much greater demand for coppice products than in modern times. Coopers used ash, elm, oak, chestnut, maple, hazel and sycamore. Ash made bowls, dishes and roof spars and was elastic enough for hoops. Gates were made of best old larch and pine. Beech was scarce but made chair legs. Springy ash provided many tools, cleft axeshafts, scythes, hayrakes, as well as cartshafts, ladder rungs and roofspars. The cordlike fibres of hazel and the ease with which it could be split provided a material that could be bent and tied. The Langdon forester of 1568 still had wood perquisites and ran from his Broxa barn a timber yard and workshop supplying boards, ash-spars, bowls and dishes. Oak lingered in use for wheelspokes, but it was harder to find the thick-trunked oak bearing stout limbs or forks that could readily serve the rising need of the coastal ships' carpenters, or the good oak that would contain three pair of wain blades or an axletree. In the 17th and 18th centuries, ship sawyers scoured the countryside seeking timber free from the 'rends, shakes and cups' which would cause leakage or might split when bolts and tree nails were driven through. Craftsmen went to the woods and were always on the look out for wood to suit particular needs. A good eye could tell which wood could bear the heat of tropical suns and endure the rubbing and tearing of marine life. The value of seasoning was known at York in 1356. Improving by seasoning now became a practical art. Alder clog blocks stood honeycombed to let in the air and hurdle hazel leant against trees.

Carpenters' axes still had a long back blade for dressing timber. Saws, chisels, mallets and hammers were locally made. Cleaving tools enjoyed the preference, wherever strength was needed in relation to size. Hand-cleft oak was riven more often than sawn though plough beams were taken out with a whipsaw. Wedges or mallets with an edge tool would follow the fibres leaving the natural curve of the grain to give lasting strength. Saws were reserved for level surfaces and cutting off. Surfaces were rough adzed or shaved with knife or axe.

The local dialect enshrined the rich forgotten language of the woodman. A hagg was a coppice and a haggsnare was the stool or stub from which coppice wood had been cut. Felling was done to leave a smooth stub that would not hold water. 'Stubbing' was grubbing up stumps of trees and to 'look' was to weed a young wood. 'Swarming' was climbing a tree with your legs and arms. Bark was 'sliped' from trees. Cattle topping underwood were said to 'brog' it while men cutting hedgethorns at fence height were said to 'buckhead'. 'Garsil' was thorns or brushwood used to make a dead hedge while 'fleaks' were wattles or hurdles woven with twigs. The fork of a tree was its 'breekin', the bough was a 'grain' and a hollow stem was a 'bun'. Diseased, black and turgid ash bark was termed 'beesucken'. Spires were stands of timber or upstanding young trees. Wavers were young timberlings left standing in a felled wood, while a 'stiven' was the shoot from the stool of a fallen tree. Standells are thriver trees left from a previous felling and a spring was the young wood raised from stools of felled trees. Among the many products, a 'spelk' was a thin piece of wood, a 'slot' a flat wood bar and a 'stower' round. A 'stang' was a long pole and a 'stoop' a post. Thick clubbed pieces of firewood were called cubs while a 'clog' was a log. 'Dottard' oaks were poor quality or broken-topped trees suitable for fuel. 'Crambles' were large boughs of trees after faggot wood had been cut but the faggots themselves were called kids.

THE DIVISION OF HIGH AND LOW DALBY

As Dalby gained its handful of scattered farmsteads it became more like other high dales of the North York Moors. There was a modest social life. During c1612, two tenants Arthur Gilbank and Peter Metcalf were charged with unlicensed brewing for sale and selling ale above the assize price, a common charge against alehousekeepers at the time. Drovers now passed through heading for Scarborough, perhaps contributing to their clientelle. Richard Gilbank of Dalby appears in the Thornton church register in 1648. Metcalf is said to have been one of Ambrose Pudsey's labourers but the Gilbanks were tenant farmers. One Dalby yeoman was charged at Kirkbymoorside quarter sessions in January 1655-6 with 'shooting at a quicke'.

The Pudsey family, briefly in the dale, seem to have witnessed the decay of the old Sheepcote House. They too may have had links with the Cholmeleys. Ambrose Pudsey was a Whitby recusant in 1595. Frazer assigned his interest in the herbage and pannage to Pudsey and gentleman Thomas Pudsey's widow for a time had the lease of 'one ferme house called Dalbye ferme, the house being very ruinous, with a garden and garth, containing by estimation 3 acres 2 roods'. Her farm rent was 1s 1d. With the house went 1683 acres, of which 1500 acres were 'open heath and moorish groundes, being sometime with the most of the rest, an agistment'. Some 42 acres were newly enclosed out of moor and wood and there were also the 50 acre Dalby Haggs. She assigned her interest to Dacre in 1624.

High Dalby House, probably in the early 1930s [Copyright unknown]

Setting aside the hermit close and its intakes, the rest of Dalby seems to have been divided into two parts, High and Low Dalby, about this time. Compact farms with ring fences and little overlap outside the ings would now replace the old open landscape. The occasion was possibly before Darcy assigned his lease to Thomas Hassell and William Ives in December 1632-3. Ives in the following March assigned his part to the use of Henry son of John Robinson, a manor lord at Thornton Dale. By 1650, young Ralph Hassell had secured the Robinson part, while Beatrice widow of Thomas Hassell had the other. The two branches of the family kept their interests distinct. Independent leases also brought leases of the divided Dalby Haggs to Beatrice and Ralph. A detailed survey of the divided properties was made for the custodians of the Duchy of Lancaster in 1651.

The Hassells of Dalby were a gentry family descended from a Thomas Hassell of London who had wed the French daughter of the Governor of Gravelines. His grandchildren included Thomas Hassell who settled at Dalby, living there till his death in 1639-40. There was a brother Samuel Hassell of Hutton on Derwent near Malton and a sister who married Francis Constable of Troutsdale, not too far away. Thomas and Beatrice had a son Thomas baptised at Thornton Dale on April Fool's Day 1635. A Ralph Hassell described as a 'gentleman' would die and be buried there in 1655. An earlier record of the older Thomas and Ralph comes from Coneysthorpe where the pair gathered with 20 others in September 1606 to assault the tax collectors. Beatrice Hassell also inherited a manor at Ampleforth in Ryedale, which passed to her daughters Elizabeth and Dorothy.

Several of the family made local marriages with other landed gentry. John Hassell wed Mary Hunter in 1657-8. Sam's daughter Mary wed Thomas Geere, squire of Great Barugh Manor c1650. Another Sam Hassell became husband to Catherine daughter of Isaac Fairfax of Thornton in April 1683. Thomas's widow Mrs Isabel Hassell was buried at Thornton in 1657-8. The son Thomas, described as a merchant taylor of the City of London was in 1664 made Chief Constable of Pickering Lythe and a younger Thomas became Vicar of Seamer, returning to Thornton for his burial in 1706-7. A Mrs Hassell still had some interest at Dalby up to 1735. The coat of arms of this family, registered at Malton in 1665, was fittingly 'three adders erect argent'.

Arms of Hassell

Although the monasteries had long since lost their interests near Dalby, one religious body in 1504 had gained a new interest, which it retained. Sir Edward Hastings gave his Ellerburn and Farmanby Manor and lands to the Dean and Canons of the King's Free Chapel of Windsor. They remained as manor lords but after 1620 let off their estate. The Dean and Canons of York Minister had also survived the dissolution of monasteries but they too now farmed out their interests. Ralph Hassell in 1649 was paying £32 a year for the Dean's tithes of Farmanby's 51 oxgangs, the glebe land, a cottage with a rood and two oxgangs and beastgates in the stinted pasture. His tithes of Dalby were said to be small for 'Dalby hath only 8 loads, with some little corn worth per annum £4'. Another statement of 1650 for 'Dalby hamlett' gives 'tithes etc' at the annual value of £2 and tithes of corn within five several farms in the Parish of Pickering at £9 6s 8d. The rent paid in 1678 was 'Dalby tithe £1 10s 0d, 18 acres 12s 1d, and tithe of Dalby woods 5s'. Richard Reeve had, back in 1643, held the Dalby tithe with the Marish tithe and Kingthorpe glebe for £12.

At Low Dalby, Beatrice Hassell in 1651 had a house called the Coathouse. Its lower west room was the kitchen, the middle room a buttery and milk house, while at the east end was 'a fair room called a parlour'. Upstairs were three chambers, making a very good house by the standards of the day. Some improvement would seem to have been effected since Pudsey's time. A barn and other necessary houses stood outside in a one acre site. With the house went nine closes, a hagg, three riggs used for sheep pasture and a tract of moor.

CLOSES	ACRES (A.R.P)*	LAND USE	PARCELS	ACRES (A.R.P)	LAND USE
Keldale End	4. 0. 0	Arable	Dalby Hagg	40. 0. 0	wood ground
Hemp Garth	1. 0. 30	Arable	Souther-borough Rigg	385. 0. 0	sheep pasture
Summer Close	4. 0. 0	Arable	Coatt Rigg	120. 0. 0	sheep pasture
Summer Close Bottom	5. 2. 0	Amp			
Highgate Ing	13. 0. 0	meadow	Hareborough Rigg	68. 0. 0	sheep pasture
Low Ing	11. 0. 30	meadow	The Moor	255. 0. 0	moor ground
Low Longlands	12. 3. 0	meadow			
Upper Longlands	13. 0. 0	Arable	Dalby Hagg	40. 0. 0	wood ground
Paddock	2. 1. 18	meadow			

*A.R.P: Acres, roods and perches

John Boyes, as Beatrice's undertenant had a house called Flaxdale End with just two rooms which were 'open to the roof' - a good description of the old local cruck-type house where the fire smoke lost itself in the rafters. With it went these closes.

Below the house	1. 2. 0 (A.R.P)	meadow
East Garth	0. 2. 5	meadow
North Garth	1. 0. 0	meadow
Tupp Close	9. 0. 0	meadow

3 Flaxdale End Closes	4. 0. 0	arable
Intake or		
Summer Cow Pasture	40. 0. 0	pasture.

The two farms together made up 935 acres 3 roods 38 perches, and paid a rent of £5 6s 8d. It was argued that on improvement it could be worth a further £69 6s 0d. Within the area were 810 standells and old dotterells worth £14 5s 4d.

Ralph Hassell's High Dalby of 1651 was in three holdings, the first no longer kept in hand and apparently without a house.

CLOSES	*AREA (ARP)*	*LAND USE*	*PARCELS*	*AREA (ARP)*	*LAND USE*
The Ing next Low Ing (Tenant Jas Todd)	*13. 3. 13*	*meadow*	*Cleufield Rigg (Tenant Rich Gilbank)*	*247. 0. 0*	*sheep pasture*
Haygate Ings (Tenant Chris Todd)	*19. 0. 0*	*meadow*	*Leven Hough and*		
Bouchard or Dutton Close (Tenant Wm Gilbank)	*28. 0. 0*	*meadow*	*Allerston Ridge (Tenant Rich Gilbank)*	*586. 0. 0*	*sheep pasture*
2 Upper & 2 Lower Fallows Closes (Tenant Wm Gilbank)	*8. 3. 2*	*meadow*			
Long Crooks Close	*1. 2. 0*	*meadow*	*Dalby Haggs (Tenant Rich Gilbank)*	*62. 0. 0*	*wood ground*

Richard Gilbank was tenant from Ralph of a house containing two rooms, with a barn at the end, called Sibdale End House.

2 closes above and below the way	5. 1. 0 (A.R.P)	arable
Calve close	1. 0. 0	meadow
Cross Close	4. 0. 20	meadow
Sibdale End Close	8. 0. 0	meadow
Braworth Close		meadow
Farr Close	6. 0. 0	meadow
Swardale Close	6. 2. 20	meadow

Another tenement of Ralph's was in the hands of a widow and had two rooms open to the roof, perhaps at the site of today's High Dalby House.

3 pieces near the house	1. 0. 0 (A.R.P)	
Hollow closes	3. 0. 0	meadow
2 Hareborough Rigg End Closes	3. 1. 0	arable
Calve Close	2. 3. 20	meadow

Although the last two plots were in Ralph's possession they were claimed by Mrs Hassell. Ralph's holding made some 1,010 acre 1 rood and 23 perches. It paid a rent of £5 6s 8d capable on improvement, the surveyor thought, of a further £77 13s 0d. There were 762 standells and dotterells worth £14 17s 4d.

In these Duchy leases, quarries and main timber were reserved and it is likely that some of the older quarries in the Dalby Riggs will have by now been opened to supply stone for the new house walls. Tenants were bound to keep premises in repair at their own costs but were allowed all 'bootes'. This meant timber could still be had for necessary house and fence repairs. The two 'fair coppices or haggs' that remained were by 1660 also divided between Beatrice and Ralph, their joint rent £1, though reckoned worth on improvement £5. A grant of King Charles's time had taken the haggs to William Poppell of Hull for 31 years, his £1 paid in two instalments at Michaelmas and Lady Day. He assigned his lease to Darcy and later conveyances brought them to Ralph and Beatrice. Standells were reserved, but most of the timber had been raised from the stools of timber trees formerly taken down. Beatrice held Low Spring Wood, some 61 acres 0 roods 32 perches, where there were 324 standells valued at £39 8s 6d, paying 10s. Ralph had Risestye alias Haygate Hagg, some 56acres and 24 poles where there were 192 great trees and standells worth £23 14s, he paying 10s.

The later leases show little sign of further change. They were sometimes granted before existing leases had expired. In 1641, a maid of honour, Elizabeth Howard, received the grant of a 15 year lease, to take effect on the expiry of a lease of 1604 made for 40 years, which itself took effect after the expiry of a lease of 1583-4 for 31 years. A 1660 Duchy survey says of Dalby that 'this is a large parcel of good ground with a fair and good sheep pasture containing by estimation 1 500 acres. This was demised by Mrs Elizabeth Howard to Mrs Hassell. Her Majesties grant hath eleven years yet unexpired'. Later, in King Charles II time, a Mr William Clement held High Dalby. In 1676 Thomas Hassell had the Low Dalby sheepcote, another small tenement and half the herbage and pannage, some 935 acres at £5 7s rent while Mr Clement by assignment had the other half, some 1,010 acres at £5 7s rent. The former was described as Thomas the Elder of Dalby when he transferred an Ampleforth estate to Thomas the Younger of Seamer in 1701.

NEIGHBOURS AND THEIR COMMONS

While Dalby became a dale of scattered farmsteads, its neighbours remained tied to traditional common field farming but saw other changes. One village, Kingthorpe, was beginning to collapse. A surveyor reported late in the 17th century that it 'doth appear by the ruins of some old buildings to have been much bigger than it is now, for the Chapel Garth shows the rubbish of an old Chapel. Smithy Garth and Cutler Garth do seem such trades were used there. Some say there is a Manor House and a court kept there by the Cholmeleys, lord thereof, from whom it was purchased by the Lady Carey'. Under the Lady Carey, Roxby also had fallen to the ground.

The Kingthorpe terrain was unfavourable: he said 'it is hard, dry and stony ground, the limestone rock lying so near that there is scarce soil for the plough and though the ground seem over .... with stones, yet in most summers they have very good crops, but a dry hot summer burns up both their corn and meadow of which they have but little'. Henry Brown still kept an alehouse there in 1607 and in 1616 a labourer who stole sheep was branded on his hand. Later in the century there seem to have been only some nine families at the village and it remained small, being further reduced when the Fothergill family emparked all land near the mansion, inclosed and replaced several old farms with fewer new ones late in the 18th century.

Dalby's other neighbour Ellerburn had a rather different experience. The village had always been small, its suite of fields narrowly confined within the valley. Its church provided for a wider parish including Farmanby. Though curate Robert Todd reported signs of decay in the building in 1568, and there were sometimes complaints that parishioners failed to get their due number of sermons, the small church continued to serve a parish role. Will Preston was removed to York Castle for unlicensed brewing at Ellerburn in 1610, but the next year John Shaw was judged for the same offence. Six years later, strolling players performed interludes at Ann Shaw's Ellerburn alehouse. Seth made gloves in 1611, the fulling mill was active in 1650 and early in the next century Andrew Horsley here would weave linen. A new stimulus came to Ellerburn about this time with the founding of the high and low paper mills and this new industry long kept Ellerburn busier than today's appearance might suggest.

Though small, Ellerburn could produce its feuds and factions. In 1611, three yeomen called Watson from Sheriff Hutton joined Robert Shawe, Roger Watson, Edward Elrington and spinster Margery Watson in an 'assault and affray' on Richard Wiles in the Bottom Close, rescuing three oxen that he had seized. George Fox's Quakerism found converts in the parish during the Parliament's years, probably the period when the wall painting of the last judgement over the chancel arch was covered over. The Quaker Stephen Keddy of Kingthorpe had £18 worth of goods taken for allowing a meeting at his house in 1671. The Society met at John Priestman's house in 1700 and as late as 1743, four of the parish's eighty families were Quakers. Another new movement brought more schools to the district. Lady Lumley's school at Thornton Dale was set up in 1657, its master of 1690 also serving as vicar of Ellerburn. Richard Throssell ran a petty school at Crosscliffe above Allerston c1648 and Roger Rogerson ten years later had a school at Farmanby. Men sought to read their new English bibles.

Scarcity of wood brought a new value to the turf and peat of the commons. Dalby's 'Waltermoor' was still a source for alders, underwood, 'coal', peat and turf in 1559-60. The word 'coal' remains ambiguous. In 1610-11, Sir Henry Gate was said to have a 'coal mine' somewhere in the forest and coal working is spoken of in Newton Dale. 'Moor-coal' would be worked from the late 17th century in moors north of Kirkbymoorside but pending fresh evidence, charcoal burning or peat quarrying seems more likely around Dalby. The shift to coal for house-fuel generally came later with the advent of rail-born and 'sea-coal'. In the meanwhile, turf and increasingly peat were widely used. Allerston, whose moors abut Dalby's had a twenty acre turbary as early as 1259-60 and in 1611 cuttings from there were supplied to Scarborough. A Duchy order 'concerning staff herding of cattle and digging of turf in Hawdale Rigg, Wettmoore on the waste' was made on June 9th 1597 but the source gives no details.

Turf was pared from the surface with an old sharp half-worn spade, or in later days a special turf-spade. The top grass might be burnt off in March, before the grouse nested. Burning off at Allerston occurred in the 14th and the 17th centuries. Turf cut best when wet. A line was set and the edge taken off, then a fifteen inch sod would be cut. 'Gravers' wearing leather knappers, divided it into 18 inch lengths, giving a jerk to turn the grass side up. Sods were 3 to 5 inches thick depending on the soil and its content of fibrous roots. Working steadily backwards, a man could cut five or six wagonloads in a day. After 3 or 4 weeks standing, it was led away in wagons or sledges. Farms had their own turf stacks and even 'turfhouses' and could use up to 25 wagonloads a year. Cooking could be done on a turf fire and the half-inch thick 'turf cakes' or 'sad cakes' remain a traditional local dish.

Peat burnt less brightly and more slowly than turf. It was dug from the deep peat at wet hollows and slacks or in the sphagnum bogs of the high watersheds. The blackest was reckoned the best. Cut from April to July at a face, perhaps ten foot high, and worked in two tiers, its removal left a quarry-like hollow that was returned to year after year. Winged peat spades or breast ploughs were developed by the 18th century, but how early is not known. With these, 2000 peats measuring 18 x 5 x 4 inches could be cut in a day. These were stacked to dry. A cart might hold 1000 but scuttles, barrows and sledges were also used. Peats are mentioned in Squire Hill's Dalby accounts for 1743.

Other materials were brought from the moors. Mr Hill's housebook of 1733-4 includes many small payments for things gathered from woods and moors. In November he bought honey from Mr Osbaldeston of Allerston. He paid 17s to John Dobson for 17 quarts in 1730. The moor fringe held many straw bee skeps placed on stones or in wall recesses called boles, which produced the strong heather honey. There were also payments for 12 birch besoms or brooms at 1s, 1s 4d worth of fir-cones from John Foxton in June, 3s to John Snawden for 2 pecks of walnuts, and in November, 2s to John Atkinson for getting 6 pecks of acorns. On the income side in 1743, Mr Vernon of Bishill paid £3 3s 'for the liberty of burning 380 bushels of bracken ashes at Dalby'. Small wood was gathered for dead hedging. Bilberries and cranberries went for pies. Bog myrtle made gale beer and honey could become botchet or mead. Seaves or rushes could serve as thatch. Bundles of ling were gathered by leather knee-padded lassies with a toothed sickle, who could cut 30 sheaves a day, and served for bedding stock, kindling, thatch and as besoms when bound with ashbands. Ashes from burnt turf and peat became handy manure.

Travellers on the commons may have been a little more frequent. Besides the silent drovers, there were more horse riding gentry. A young traveller over Pexton Moor c1607 was seven-year-old Hugh Cholmeley, moving house with his father and mother to Whitby. In his own words 'beginning to ride a little way by myself as we passed over a common called Pastmoor, one of my father's servants riding beside me, I had a desire to put my horse into a gallop'. He fell off and the horse trod on his hat. As an adult, Sir Hugh was made Deputy-Lieutenant and Colonel of the Train Bands for Whitby-Strand, Pickering Lythe and Scarborough. In 1639 he brought his 'whole regiment' together on Pexton Moor, west of Dalby for training, and caught a cold. During the manoeuvres, a man called Halden from Pickering gave a captain some language and Cholmeley felled him with a blow under the ear with his silver-tipped cane. The man suffered hardly from the blow and Cholmeley from remorse. In the Civil Wars between Cavaliers and Parliament, he commanded a cavalry force in several actions. Thornton Dale saw a battle and Richard Marshall of Farmanby was slain in the Parliament's service. Not long after, the inhabitants of Pickering Lythe petitioned, saying that they had sent men and lent money and horse to serve Parliament with Sir Hugh, and had then had five regiments of horse and 3000 foot billeted in the district for the siege of Scarborough, after Sir Hugh had changed allegiance to the king.

An inquisition for bounding Lockton, Allerston and Dalby had been made 18th June 1583-4. At Allerston in 1612-13 Sir Richard Egerton had a licence from the Duchy to enclose the wastes in that manor with a small ditch. Some of the Crosscliffe enclosures and farmsteads appear in the records shortly afterwards. It is possible that the square enclosure abutting Dalby Wetmoor and including the Wet Moor and Red Dykes was made at this time. Controlled pasturing or even early rabbit warrening may have been in prospect. Allerston's warren is the earliest locally known but it was later given a warren house much closer to the village. He also made enclosures at Blackhowe. Similar enclosures seem to have been made for farming northeast of Lockton in the 17th Century, spreading farmsteads into north Staindale. Thornton and Farmanby's high commons remained unaffected, the only encroachment being some pest houses built for plague victims on Thornton Moor in 1638.

John Hill had surveys made of the commons. On 28th March 1742, the surveyor wrote, 'I began surveying the commons behind the paper mills and to Loft Moor to Stonneygate. The lordships either side have encroached. The town shepherds who have not property enough to believe it make use often of their tongues and dogs. There have been several contests between Wilton and Thornton shepherds. Kingthorpe have encroached'. He measured Whitecliffe Rigg between Willowdale and Eckdale from the beck near Flainsey House to Sandale, with Christopher Smales and his son carrying the chains for 8d and 6d a day. Then he did the small ridge running from the bottom of Sandale to the top of Dalby completing Thornton Common east of the beck. Another letter from Joseph Studholme to Hill says he had surveyed the east end of Whitecliffe, describing it as bounded south by Sandale, north by Eckdale and east by 'Allerston dyke, which was made by the Egertons when that lordship belonged to them'. He went on to Thornton Wetmoor, bounded north-west by Flainsey Ridge, south by Allerston Dyke and north by a road which runs along the side of Dalby enclosure, the dyke and enclosure meeting at a place called 'Adderston or rather Edgerton Nook'. He then went down the dale that divided Southerbrough, belonging to Dalby, from Flainsey Ridge. He asked for some large paper to make a map on.

4

DALBY - NEW WAYS OF FARMING

Because Dalby had one owner rather than several and but a handful of tenants on short leases rather than the mixture of tenures that characterised many common field townships, it was always susceptible to farming changes should anyone wish to pioneer them. Only the unpromising character of much of the higher soil limited its possibilities. The early enclosure of the valley land in small closes had affected only a small proportion of the whole. Woods still accounted for some but most was sheep pasture. Yet the very character of the high sheepwalks would foster dramatic changes in land use. The good valley pastures allowed early stock breeding in small fields while other townships were still reliant on a township bull set to a communal herd. The rough high ground proved ideally suited to farming a new stock, rabbits, along with the traditional sheep.

Innovations require innovators. The Hill family first gained a local interest at Farmanby by tenanting the Dean and Chapter of Windsor's manor in c1620, but a more substantial investment was made in the early Restoration years. In 1668-9, John Hill of Normanby acquired a new Farmanby lease and bought the main Thornton Dale manor, which had lately belonged to Lady Lumley. In 1669-88 he bought another Thornton manor and in 1679 more land from John Dutton at Thornton and Farmanby. Several more small properties were bought up at these townships and in 1678, Mr Hill acquired not only the Stewardship of the Honour of Pickering but an assignment of the lease of the castle and manor of Pickering, which made him lessor of the interests of the Duchy of Lancaster throughout the entire district of the old Forest of Pickering.

Of considerable wealth - he paid £2,293 16s 8d for the Lumley manor alone - Hill had legal and estate experience. Tradition claims that his family fortune was founded in the merchanting of silk and the family had London mercantile connections. After his death in 1695 at the age of 78, he was followed by a son John, who had been settled at Thornton when he married the wealthy Grace Legard of a London and Ganton mercantile family in 1678. The father and son made considerable innovations. After amalgamating some of the Thornton estates, they began negotiations for an enclosure in 1669. In 1678 a chancery decree was obtained for enclosing the Farmanby and West Thornton open fields, while leaving the commons, including Pexton Moor and Greencliff towards Dalby, as open moor. Both the son and the grandson continued the policy of making further acquisitions and improvements on Thornton-Farmanby estates.

The first innovations came on the Farmanby property, which included much of Ellerburn. Dalby, as part of the Duchy estate, was already in lease and the lessors had sub-tenants now at both High and Low Dalby. John Robinson, a Lockton yeoman, and his sons William and Thomas took a six year tenancy from the Reverend Thomas Hassell of Seamer of the Sheepcoat House, 935 acres of herbage and pannage and all the tenements standing on them in June 1702. Their rent was £87. The lease had the usual clauses reserving great trees, underwoods, mines and quarries. Hassell provided haybote, hedgebote, ploughbote and cartbote and the tenants had to repair hedges, ditches, houses, fences and closes. The tenants' freedom to innovate was limited by clauses requiring written licence from Hassell before they pared, burned or ploughed up any meadow or pasture, or the closes below the cliff 'apart from that already bounded for tillage'. Low Dalby was still being farmed by Thomas Robinson in 1718 and by his widow in April 1739. Meanwhile another Lockton family had tenanted High Dalby which by now had a farmhouse. John Boddy was there before his death in 1681. He was followed by Robert Boddy, mentioned in 1719, John Boddy (1722, 1739), Robert Boddy (1751, 1755), Francis Boddy (1755), Edward Boddy (1816), Robert Boddy (1825), Edward Boddy (1830) and John Boddy (1866, 1886).

Besides the leasehold estates, there was the Duchy copyhold 'house and close called Keldhouse or the Hermitage Close lying in the Manor of Pickering on the south end of Dalby, on the east side of Farmanby Common'. In 1722, it was differently described as 'Keldhousegarth, which lies near Ellesborne, (the house is down), containing about 4 acres, and now belongs to Mr James Boyes of Thornton in his own occupation – all of it is said not to be copyhold'.

It was the younger John Hill who turned his attention to Dalby. His rental there in 1733 included the Queen's rent of £10 14s, the Dalby Haggs rent of £8 and a Dalby rent that he had acquired in reversion of £188. The Queen's rent was due for renewal in 1735. In January of that year, when Thomas Robinson lay very ill, he made enquiries about James Boyes' house. The dale, with the deer gone, the woodland reduced to narrow belts along the valley sides, the high riggs offering sheep pasture and home for wild birds, and with the valley pastures, was the Duchy property closest to his Thornton estate and looked ripe for conversion to an improved kind of farming.

PIONEERING NEW INDUSTRY AT ELLERBURN

The startling innovation on the Hill estate was of quite a different kind. It brought the new and rare industry of paper-making to the small village of Ellerburn. We cannot be sure that it had not begun early in the 17th century but it is first mentioned in March 1680 when a son was born to William Warren of an Ellerburn Paper Mill. William Long was working another called the White Paper Mill by 1696. Earlier paper-makers and mills in Yorkshire are only known at Old Byland, mentioned in 1615, and in the West Riding - Sheepscar 1660, Monk Bretton 1666, and Norton 1656, with later references there at Thorp Arch 1683, Ryther 1684, Owlerton 1689, Brightside 1700 and Halifax 1701. White paper making was particularly rare and needed fine linen rags to make the best papers. Coarse rags and other flax and hemp materials went to make the commoner papers.

Though the mills stood virtually alone in north-east Yorkshire, it is not clear whether any substantial local source of demand for paper existed. Through the nation, demand was rising and supplies from France were often interrupted in the second half of the century. Immigration of French makers is thought to have fostered white paper making. Nor is it clear who made the initial investment. Though the process was simple, equipment was expensive. An existing mill could have been adapted, for Ellerburn had long had a fulling mill, but it was still active and the paper mills were built further upstream. The steady flow of hard pure clean water from the Dalby valley, essential for white paper, would be a factor in choosing the site but the ready supply of good rags from the expanding Ryedale and Pickering Lythe linen manufacture, operating at least since the early 17th century, must have been decisive. A possible family link may be relevant. An Endymion Porter was one of the very few white-paper makers in England in 1640. The three bells of the Porter family formed part of the Hill family coat of arms and a memorial to John Porter, a London merchant who died in 1686, is in Thornton Dale Church.

Nothing is known about the early Ellerburn mills. The process in use at the time saw rags sorted, washed and retted and then pounded to pulp in troughs of water called mortars. The pounding hammers were driven by a water wheel. The resulting pulp went into a vat of lukewarm water, from which the vat man formed sheets of paper singly by inserting a wire-mesh mould and shaking it to form a matted layer. After a number of sheets had been made, they were pressed to exclude water, hung on lines to dry and then sized, if to be used for writing.

The High Mill was rebuilt by Mr Hill in 1733 using 170 oak trees that cost £22 and another 21 ton of oak wood and some deals. It was given a tiled roof and walls of Ebberston Stone. The oak axle tree was 73 foot long. Mr Warren was tenant of both mills in 1734, followed by his son William from 1748 to 1778. Meanwhile a William Long, paper-maker, insured the Bell Mill at Great Driffield in 1754. In 1748 April, Mr Hill's steward wrote 'there is a call for all sorts of paper'. The men were being paid 5s a week till May Day and 6s thereafter and were in constant employment. Whether the Hollander beating engine was installed is not known. Use of bleaches allowed wider ranges of paper to be made and Ellerburn had a bleach mill rebuilt in 1748. Ellerburn was certainly capable of making writing and printing paper of all sorts towards the end of the 18th century 'which for colour and quality equalled any that could be made' and 'house–covering paper'. By then a number of other Yorkshire mills had been established.

From 1778 to 1811 Thomas Campion ran the High Mill and James Nicholls was at Low Mill, which was renovated in 1789 but kept some old cruckbeams. Up to 80 hundredweight of paper a year was produced by George Nicolls c1817 and Thomas Fell made boxes in 1829. Richard Nicholls was at Low Mill c1833. Thomas Maraden kept High Mill till c1869 about which time it became a farm. Wagons are said to have taken the paper to Pickering, returning with rags collected by 'ragmen'. George Pickering, the last known paper-maker, was apprenticed in 1865 at Low Mill. He worked in a rag-sorting shed standing across the road from the farm. He died in 1927 at Thornton Dale and in his time a machine tore up the rags. Closure was attributed to competition from West Riding and other steam mills with their better supplies of rags. The local linen trade faded in the early decades of the 19th century.

The date of demise of the other Ellerburn mill, used for making cloth, is not exactly known. Wool, hemp and linen weaving of coarse cloth had been a small scale local industry for centuries. Ellerburn had a fulling mill in 1335. On a famous occasion back in 1497, Sir Roger Hastings, accompanied by 20 others armed with bills and bows attending Ellerburn Church, had threatened to slay the fuller Ralph Joyner who was inside. He had to make his escape to Pickering across the hills. In 1650 at least five hemp yards were kept in the village and the mill was still active. Probably it was the same as the farm and 'bleach mill' held by Richard Marshall c1743 and John Marshall in 1741. It was rebuilt in 1748, when the Hill steward reported that 'Foster wants deals and an ash tree out of Marshall's warren or any other of the Dean's wood for his cloth mill, a tree about 20ft of timber will do.' It was planned the next year to make the ground between the two paper mills, called Game Acre, into a bleach garth. Hemp and flax were retted ready for use by spreading the straw on the ground, or soaking in pits, so that water rotted away perishable parts and left the durable fibres for the coarse linen manufacture, which expanded in the late 16th century. Finished cloths were also hung out to bleach and as many as 40 webs are said to have stretched in the field. Richard Kirk kept the mill and bleach grounds in 1785 followed by Thomas Rogers c1818, about the time that local flax-growing was in decline.

THE NEW RABBIT WARRENS

Rabbit rearing on a large scale was also pioneered at Ellerburn before being developed in Dalby. The idea was not novel but the scale of approach was. Small warrens had been kept in the Middle Ages. Sir Roger Hastings in c1498 had been accused of making a two-acre coney warren somewhere in Thornton or Farmanby out of arable land. Another small early warren may be remembered in the name 'Coney Warren' on Staindale Rigg north of Dalby. Conies were simply old rabbits. Large-scale warrens had been developed in the late 17th century. In 1659, forty-eight Pickering yeomen were accused of taking 1000 rabbits from a warren of the queen at Middlehead. A Thornton Dale yeoman poached in a local warren in 1693.

Yet, the new warrens were not so much hunting preserves, in the old sense of the word, as breeding farms.

Ellerburn and Dalby had suitable land available. That at Ellerburn was small, with an area of common behind it, where others had common rights. That at Dalby was extensive but let off by lease. One yearly tenant at Ellerburn had 'a barren sandy bank called Skeath Woods and a parcel of coppice called the Ellars'. This was Richard Marshall. It is not clear whether he or Squire Hill took the initiative, but before October 1733 it had become a warren. In 1734, Mr Hill paid masons £1 for 20 days work at 'warren house'. He paid the land tax on Ellerburn Warren in 1741 and in a note of 1743 recorded that Marshall had a mountainous piece of ground called Seathwood and Ellers turned into a coney warren of some 20 acres. Hill clearly made improvements but in 1733 Marshall was already supplying rabbit meat to Thornton Hall while working part time as a carrier. Mr Hill paid him 8s for eight couple of summer rabbits, 1s 6d for leading stone and lime and 12s for leading coals from Scarborough. He often did other work on the estate. Another man Roger Coates also supplied '30 couple of rabbits at 8d each' in March 1733-4 and a lot of 16 couple was bought for 13s 4d in October. A youth called the 'rabbit boy' was also employed as messenger, fetching cheese from York for 6d or a parcel from the village for 2d. Ellerburn Warren was the old type, close to the village, with natural woodland and undergrowth. It was less favoured than sites that would later be used, but did share in the warmer valley temperature. It was probably abandoned in the face of the larger ones developed further north, for in 1797 Skeathwood was 'late a coney warren'.

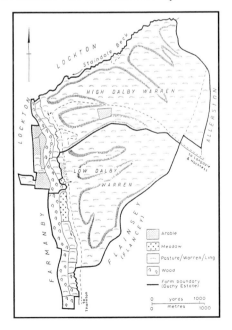

The Dalby Estate of the Duchy Of Lancaster, c 1776, from 'The Rabbit Warrens of the Tabular Hills, North Yorkshire' by A Harris and S A Spratt, Yorkshire Archaeological Journal, Vol 63, 1991. [By kind permission of the Yorkshire Archaeological Society]

Flainsey Rigg was also converted to a warren. It may have been worked by Roger Coates in 1733 and certainly existed along with Low Dalby warren before 1743. Whatever may have existed before, Low Dalby and Flainsey warrens were improved by Squire Hill. He had surveys made in 1742 and re-organised both in the next year. On 20th March 1742 Mr Bean and William Dowthwaite received £3 7s 6d for their board. Mr Jenner the surveyor from Windsor was also a visitor in April 1743. An earlier warren had probably been developed on the nearby Allerston moors earlier in the 17th century and provided a model. With the Dalby lease in hand after 1735 it was possible to exploit the new realisation that rabbits would increase quickly on land supporting only a few sheep, provided that there was some undergrowth to support the breeding stock. Warmth is life to rabbits in winter and the sloping riggs of Dalby and Flainsey offered a broad warm southerly aspect. Digging with their forepaws, rabbits like a slope to burrow in and there was dry soil on the limestone away from the peat bogs. The areas were broad enough to offer a good return from a large stock.

John Hill II died in 1738 and it was his son, another John, who carried through the new developments at Dalby. Serving as Customs Commissioner till his resignation in 1747 to become MP for Higham Ferrers, he took out a new grant of the Honour and Manor of Pickering in 1739. Often away from his estate, he nonetheless managed it by closely supervising his stewards, until his death in 1753. Hill seems to have taken over direct farming of the warrens in December 1742. He then paid Roger Coates' work bill of £1 14s 9d, and also £52 10s for '900 couple of rabbits left upon Flainsey, more than he entered upon, at 14d the couple'. In May 1743, he also paid John and Thomas Robinson for '1843 couple of rabbits on Dalby at Lady Day, 1743, at 11d the couple' making £84 9s 5d. He gave them a further £8 8s for their nets, belts, traps and spades, setting against it £10 received from them for repairs of Dalby Farm and for 160 couple of rabbits wanting of the number they entered upon at Flainsey at Lady Day 1742, valued £7 6s 8d at 11d the couple. John Robinson as tenant of Flainsey Warren had paid £63 8s 0d a year rent.

Establishing a first class warren was not easy. Stock might have to be dug in to help them settle. A bad winter could give heavy loss. Miss Hill wrote to her Uncle John in March 1744 that Marshall was unwilling to take the ings and woods at their old rent 'as so many rabbits had been killed off'. It is possible that Dalby and Flainsey were first run as open warrens. Walling was desirable to keep out poachers and vermin, and to keep rabbits in, but was expensive and any investment took some time to recover. Squire Hill wrote to his neighbour, the Quaker John Priestman in January 1746 saying 'it is my desire that you would not let your tenants under pretexts of looking after your sheep go out at unreasonable hours, at eleven o'clock at night, with dogs trained to kill game, for fear of being deluded by bad company to kill coneys or do other mischief'.

In the previous year, there had been a clamour against Priestman when 'labouring families had lost their all' due to dogs suspected of being his, having killed over 20 sheep on the common. The event had given Hill's warrener 'a strong suspicion'. Hill ordered Brown to keep down the rabbits that strayed from the warren onto the common so that there could be 'no complaint of losing by warrens'. Rabbits came there from Allerston and other warrens anyway. The squire now hastened to assure Priestman that he did not suspect him of getting them for himself and offered that if he or any of his neighbours wanted a couple at any time, they were welcome.

For some years, the squire worked the warrens directly. He paid John Robinson £4 10s as 15 weeks' wages and board up to Michaelmas 1743, as well as 1s 6d 'hiring pennys for two warreners to kill at Dalby'. In November he paid the warreners John Bowes and Thomas Brown, 18s and £1 respectively as a month's wages up to November 10th. In October he had spent 7s buying three ferrets for Dalby and 4s 6d for a 'rabbit dog'. Yet John Brown seems to have tenanted one Dalby warren in c1746. John Hawkswell who visited him in March said that he never knew a worse winter in his own warren, probably at Allerston, but of Dalby commented 'Brown will do there. There was a good stock of rabbits left after the killing season. If Brown doesn't run into arrears, there is stock of sheep and other goods always upon the ground which will secure half a year's rent'. The new tenant had enough old hay and he had advised him to let off as much of his meadow that year as he could. In May, Mr S Hill wrote that 'Brown's warren has not suffered so much as feared by the severe weather'. Dalby hedges were in good order and there were a 'good many vermin hung up'.

Joseph Studholme was commissioned to survey the commons from Thornton Fields to Flainsey in March 1746, perhaps as a prelude to fencing. Robert Smithson and other tenants pressed Hill in February 1749 about stoups and rails for fencing the warren from the common, and asked if he wanted any of the fallen trees in the warren for that purpose. The Dalby warrens were probably bounded in 1743. In 1777 the fenced part of Flainsey was 304 acres 1 rood 10 poles in extent but in 1785 Nuttall Frank tenanted 373 acres 3 roods 17 poles called Flainsey Warren for £60 a year. High Dalby Warren included 972 acres 3 roods 18 poles and Low Dalby Warren 792 acres 24 poles. Most of the old sheepwalk was included but in fact sheep still seem to have been allowed in with the rabbits.

Warrening could be a profitable use of poor land. There were losses to fox and hawk, and in snow, but the dry-soiled riggs gave a good fur and meat in November and severe climate brought on a fine thick fur. A spell of dry weather, before and after the early spring breeding, gave faster growth. Rabbits were unable to dig snow so warreners put out ashboughs to give shelter and left dumps of gorse and heaps of hay in small enclosures for food. Extra feed might also prove necessary at breeding time for the young at early spring, and late summer, if animals were not killed early. The warrener culled weak rabbits and to foster the stock might protect breeding does in a hut. Rabbit generations would stay in limits of territories marked out with scent and fluid but breeding growth could cause spread, especially if there was a lack of cover. Over time droppings could sour the ground and, with intensive grazing, could extinguish many species, the land becoming 'rabbit-sick'. It could be remedied with a harrow.

Warren 'fencing' seems chiefly to have been by grass sods. They were cheaper than stone or wood. Walls, two sods wide, of 16 x 12 inches, might rise to 6 feet high, capped with furze, thorn or turf. Hard weather escapes over snow drifts could hardly be stopped but escape holes made in drought could be blocked by the warrener. Good walling made harvesting easier. The early warrener's way of bolting with a ferret and catching by trap, snare or net remained the ways of the poacher but as the warrens were properly laid out, the 'rabbit type' became the normal way of harvesting. In the early day at Dalby, ferrets, a spaniel bought at Whitby, and large nets were used, but at an unknown date, an elaborate network of types was created. The usual 'type' was a stone lined hole covered with a trapdoor, either placed in a small walled enclosure or on a pathway between burrows and feeding grounds. The trapdoor was a drop-board balanced to tip the rabbit down into the hole. In the more sophisticated types, the drop-board axle worked with a wheel and pinnion that moved for each fall so that the trap could be set for a required number and to avoid smothering. In the later days, turnips were put in the enclosures for autumn and winter feed along with tree branches called 'garsell'. Coats achieved their best condition after the autumn moult and most were taken between November 5th and Christmas or Candlemas.

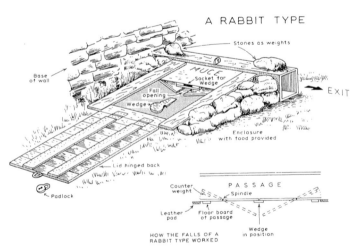

A rabbit type as shown by T P Horner in Vol 17 of 'Dalesman', 1955.
[By kind permission of Dalesman Publishing]

By 1817, the Dalby warrens were part of a belt of warrens that had filled a large corner of newly enclosed commons running eastwards over the limestone hills. Over 6000 acres here were stocked with rabbits. The Reverend George Young of Whitby writing in that year said that the largest were Dalby (1700 acres), Dalby (1100), Allerston (1200), Scamridge (700), High Scamridge (400), Cockmoor Hall, Snainton (300) and Troutsdale (400). Others included the Langdale End warren and the Lockton warren laid down in the 18th century, of 400-500 acres. Each of the large warrens then sold several thousand skins annually, at 1s to 2s a couple, to the hatters of Scarborough, Whitby, Pickering, Malton and York. The carcasses went for meat.

Rabbit marketing was subject to some changes of method and considerable fluctuation in price. A letter of 24th October 1744 tells of how 'George Brown has sold together half of his rabbits to Locksmith of Pickering at 12d the couple but must take them to Bollington which will make the price little more than 9d the couple'.

Steward William Willmot told Squire Hill in February 1749 'I apprehend the rabbits will pay pretty well and similarly the skins because we did not this year, as usual, sell the slaughter to any one particular person, but sold the carcasses in the markets, though not at so good prices as they have been some years upon account of the great quantities of butcher's meat being killed off (due to cattle distemper), though I imagine the skins will turn out very well. He paid me £80 lately'. This suggests that skinning was done locally and this was later normal, the skins being dried, before sale to furriers and hatters. It was essential if a quick move to market could not be made. A cottage at Ellerburn had racks for drying skins, a store of nets, traps and lanterns, and a store of turnips for winter feed, but the 'warren house' at Dalby has not been identified. Masons spent 20 days at one warren house in October 1734 at 12d a day, a bill of £1. Various small buildings occur in the warren area in 1777.

In later days, hucksters bought entire lots, moving them quickly to market inside covered carts fitted with tiers of rods to string the rabbits on. A note in Mr Hill's papers states that 'the following is the prices that rabbit skins sold for'.

In	1810	at	12s	the dozen	1817	at	8s	1824	at	7s 6d
	1812		11s		1818		13s	1825		7s 6d
	1812		14s 6d		1819		10s	1826		6s 9d
	1813		16s		1820		9s	1827		5s
	1814		16s 6d		1821		7s 6d	1828		5s
	1815		15s		1822		9s	1829		6s
	1816		14s		1823		9s	1830		5s 6d

The high price era ended with the close of the Napoleonic Wars but it could still be said in 1817 that rabbits were the most profitable use for the dry limestone land. Costs were small and sheep were kept on the same ground. Three thousand acres might produce 7000 to 20000 rabbits in a year, the does breeding five or six times. Five or six hundred couples could be slaughtered in a night.

IMPROVING FARM STOCK BY BREEDING

Just as John Hill altered land use in the high ground so he altered the character of farming down below. He improved the farms and restocked them. His rental of 1738-9 shows his initial return from the dale.

TENANT	RENT 1738-9	RENT 1741	RENT 1742-3
Robert Boddy for Upper Dalby Farm	£90	£90	£85
John & Thomas Robinson and their mother. Low Dalby Farm	£100	£100	£100
Roger Coates 2 closes, parcel of Dalby	£10	£10	£10 (late Coates)
Christopher Simpson	£10	£10	-
Lady Day Total	£210	£210	£195

Improving hedges and fencing of the dale enclosures and dividing the warren from the farms was a prelude to restocking. A new cattle house may also have been made. Potatoes were planted, and a new area fenced for turnips during 1743. Labourers taken on by the estate did all this work. In 1737, at Thornton, they were paid 6d from Martinmas to Lady Day, 7d from Lady Day to May Day and 8d from May Day to Martinmas. Wrights and thatchers received 12d and joiners 14d. The common labourer was expected to do a wide variety of tasks. In 1742, Dalby saw a little hedging, paid at 8s 2d. The next year, a great deal more was done.

Work at Dalby in 1743

		£	s	d
April	Labourers hedging in Dalby	1	5	3
	Labourers at Dalby	1	1	4
	Hedgers and moulders at Dalby	1	17	8
	Labourers hedging at Dalby	1	4	10
May	Expenses about ploughing ground manuring it and planting it with potatoes	5	3	10
	Labourers fencing there	2	0	10
	30 load of stone at haggs got up	10	0	0

		£	s	d
	Labourers at Dalby		6	8
	Labourers at Dalby			8
June	Labourers at Dalby		14	0
	Thatcher at Dalby		8	4
	Thatch & thatching at Dalby	3	10	6
May	Draught work at Dalby	1	13	2
	Labourers		11	10
July	Labourers at Dalby fencing in the turnip ground		19	6
	4 chains at Dalby		4	0
	3lb of hemp for net yarn and spinning it		2	5
November	Masons		7	2

The potatoes were taken up in November at a cost of £1 17s 10d and John Priestman spent 'two days leading them'.

The Squire had bought a breeding bull for Dalby back in 1734 when the old black cattle were the dominant breed in the district. Now he bought some Scotch cows.

Restocking Dalby 1743

		£	s	d
May	To Thomas Parks for 9 Scotch cows at 45s apiece to stock Dalby, and a bull 35s	22	0	0
	To John Priestman, for 13 Scotch cows at 46s	29	18	0
September	A milk cow	4	0	0
October	To John Gilbank, for a black heifer, stock at Dalby	19	6	0

Income from Dalby herd 1743

		£	s	d
August	From George Todd, for Scotch calves sold at Dalby	1	5	9
	John Nicholson, a Scotch cow	2	10	0
September	4 oxen sold to Kirkby fair	28	19	8½
	yearlings sold to John Priestman		15	0
	black heifer sold to Richard Scales	2	9	0
October	calves sold to George Todd	3	16	3

An incidental reference to 'geist' cattle suggests that outsiders may still have been bringing beasts to pasture at Dalby.

The old local breeds of sheep were a 'thin carcassed, ill formed, white faced hornless breed' in the vales and the black or mottle faced, hardy coarse-wooled moorland sheep. It is not clear what breed John Hill bought in 1743 but he went a long way to get them. They may have been Teeswaters, the so-called 'mud' sheep, well-fleshed and coarse-wooled, or the Scotch sheep, popular a little later.

Sheep purchases 1743

		£	s	d
June	bought 175 wethers at Slagshaw at 7s 8d	67	0	0
	105 wether hags at 4s 8d	24	10	0
	160 wether hags 8s	64	0	0
	173 wether hags 8s 8d	74	0	0
	toll at Corbrig		10	2
	to drivers on the road and watching in the night	1	10	0
	to John Hawkswell & S Tetlay expenses to and from, 4 nights out	1	7	8
	Total	£232	17	0
October	200 ewes at 6/-	60	0	0
	120 ewes at 4s 4d	26	0	0
	120 wethers	36	0	0
	2 tups for Dalby from Margaret Watson	1	3	6
	6 tups	2	5	0
	toll		1	6
	John Hawskell & Steward's expenses 8 days out	1	18	8
	Total	£129	8	8

Sales 1743

		£	s	d
October	400 wethers	100	0	0
	81 yearlings	22	0	0
	20 small rigills and 21 casual sheep	2	2	3
	rigills	6	6	0
	80 wethers	28	5	0
	from Robert Boddy from a tup sold of Dalby	1	0	0
November	casual sheep sold at Dalby to Thomas Crosby		2	6
	of Lockton			
	50 sheep sold at Dalby to Robert Lyth	18	2	6
	casual ewe sold to Richard Crosby		2	6

Such attempts to improve the stock would spread through the district but in most townships needed enclosure before much progress could be made. Previously the dales had reared their own stock. About 1796, Mr Hill kept a prize bull for the use of his tenants at Thornton to assist improvement of their stock. Cattle were now given more attention. Steward and squire discussed in January 1748 whether two oxen forward in flesh should be kept in the field and take the spring season at grass, or whether to 'take them into the house' immediately and give them corn and hay. In that year distemper became widespread. In anticipation, Robert Champley and others sought a place distant from the villages to put diseased cattle. Flainsey House was suggested for the 'convenience of the water, if not detrimental to George Brown in taking them in'. Milk cows were given the best that was available in summer pasture and winter hay. The squire had his own haystack in Dalby Ing, usually sold off later in the century, by which time the Hills' direct stocking of Dalby had probably ceased. Young cattle, or yearlings were housed the first winter, with hay, and taken to as good a summer pasture as was available. By the close of the century, far more beef was butchered and more beef eaten as a result of improved fatting, but much was still salted and hung for winter provision.

More ewes were put to the ram in late November or early December to delay lambing beyond the worst snows. Breeding ewes were docked in early spring. In autumn, sheep were salved to kill lice, prevent scab and to aid wool growth, a mixture of poor butter and tar being used. Mutton suet was put in to stiffen it if the weather was warm. Ewes wintered on turnips or grass and in snow a man might ride to the moor making tracks so that the heath could be reached. As with cattle, the increase of winter fodders consequent on enclosure allowed much more flexible management of flocks. New breeds produced better wool, finer grained mutton and sheep fatter at two years than old stock had been at three. Washing and shearing days were country occasions. A man might shear sixteen large sheep or thirty moor sheep in a day. Expenses at a July sheep washing and clipping were £1 7s 6d while 12s 4d was spent on sheep greasing at Dalby. Sixteen pounds of tallow and some butter for sheep salve cost £1 4s 4d. Some 4s went to Matthew Crosby that same month 'for bringing five sheep to waif and crying them'. In September the shepherd was paid 13 weeks board at 2d a week till Michaelmas, while Crosby tended the sheep for 12 weeks on Flainsey in November for 12s. Mowing, haymaking and stacking were paid for in November. In 1745 Bartle Pickering was paid 2s for a day leading wood from Dalby and 2s for a day leading hay in the intacks.

NEW PLANTATIONS AND OLD COPPICE

The immediate tenant of the Duchy of Lancaster was responsible for maintaining its properties and could use timber within the old forest bounds for the purpose. With growing timber shortage, the trees to be used for house repair were marked out by Crown surveyors and only small wood could be had free of supervision. The lessor in turn controlled woodland use by his tenants. Leases commonly specified what could be had in some detail. The lessor's estate steward and his bailiff's courts continued to exercise control of the tenantry. Abel Tassin D'Allome's lease of the local Duchy interests in 1697 required him to repair 'houses, buildings, walls, hedges, ditches, mounds, banks and enclosures … taking houseboot and timber by appointment of the King's Surveyor-General, but hedgeboot, plowboot, fireboot and cartboot, without delivery, doing no waste, to be used on the premises and not elsewhere'. The Hill family as Duchy lessors were similarly bound.

On their own estates, landlords were now actively conserving woodland by enclosure, to exclude grazing animals, and extending it by new plantations. The new squire at Thornton Dale, John Hill, began planting there in 1737-8 when his steward Sam Tetley sent a man and two horses to fetch 3600 young trees. Two March days later, he brought 4000 more. Neither origin nor destination is precisely known but there was an immediate problem of finding nursery space for them to grow. Some of the Thornton and Farmanby house garths were used. Plantings were made in 1742, including some at Marshall's Bottom. Payments in the labourers' accounts for 1746 include some to women for weeding nurseries. In March, Mary Keddy and Sarah Watson were 'together four days weeding the young beeches in the nursery on the other side of the new road and weeding the young quickwood behind the rails at the north end of Peaselands'. Robert Eaman had a day mending fences in Low Plantation. Winter planting in 1748-9 included spruce, fir, ash, beech, hazel, box hedge and oak. Some elms from the kitchen garden and some firs from Peaselands were taken up for replanting.

As the project prospered, the squire received requests for young trees from his neighbours. In 1749 Mr Harding desired ten Scotch firs and Robert Smithson asked for ten young ash trees to plant. Their estates were at Pickering and Kirkby Misperton. Parson Wyke of Levisham asked for half a score of fir trees to set round his house there, our first record of a planted shelter belt. Mr Ward wanted some elm and beech but the Steward wrote 'We may spare some beech. As to elms I don't know where we have any young ones, except what are growing out of the stools by way of layers, which at this time, February 1748-9, are improper to transplant'. Even Hill had to buy oaks. For rebuilding the Ellerburn High Paper Mill he bought 170 oak trees for £22 from William Robinson of Kirkbymoorside and 21 ton of oak wood at £7 from Deepdale from the Duchy. Brian Fenwick received £5 for one large oak tree containing 73 foot to serve as the mill's axletree. Some deal was used and other timber brought from Welburn and Helmsley.

In his Duchy leasehold estates, Hill's problems were very different. There is no record of plantations yet but the early 18th century surveys of the woodland suggest that a hundred years of coppice management had effected some improvement. Nonetheless, large trees were in desperately short supply. John Hill probably gained control of the Dalby Haggs in 1735 when a Duchy survey of the timber was made and a warrant issued for felling. A letter from his steward Sam Tetley in January argued 'the sooner you come to a resolution about the wood, the better, on account of bark, which will go sooner this year than usually by reason of the open weather'. The 'total contents of timber trees growing in Dalby Haggs belonging to the Honourable John Hill Esq', as numbered and marked IH, when inspected and marked by John Wooler and John Baynes on November 12th,' was 750 trees containing 369 tuns.

The Content of Timber Trees growing in Dalby Hags. 1735
(began at north end of Lyddigate Hag)

1	14	0	51	15	0	1	11	2	51	13	1
2	8	2	52	10	0	2	18	0	52	18	7
3	8	7	53	15	0	3	15	1	53	23	2
4	25	0	54	25	6	4	11	0	54	19	0
5	9	4	55	11	2	5	13	4	55	26	2
6	13	1	56	16	5	6	18	5	56	22	0
7	17	5	57	12	4	7	10	0	57	14	4
8	9	4	58	15	2	8	12	3	58	13	7
9	7	0	59	31	4	9	16	0	59	29	7
10	9	0	60	11	2	10	27	6	60	23	2

An extract from the survey of several hundred trees. The total of 16 399.0 had 'bark to deduct' of 1 639, leaving 14 760.0 divided by 40 to make 369 tuns.

When John Wooler returned on 31 August 1739 to review the trees he re-marked and numbered them afresh with black paint but found 39 were broken and blown down by 'storm of wind that happened about the beginning of November'. On a review of 31 December, he found 16 small unmarked oak trees blown down, of little value for anything but tenants' boots, though containing about 96 solid feet. He also found six trees that had been marked twice over by mistake. In December 1748 he found number 718 blown down and numbers 460, 463 and 586 missing, though their stools were found. He blackpainted those whose numbers were defaced.

Repairs, rebuilding and new building at Dalby itself took some trees but housebote was becoming a real problem. With the scarcity of full-grown timber, it was almost grudgingly allowed. Mr S Hill wrote in May 1746 that 'I told John Baines repeatedly to be careful in measurement of the wood at Dalby and haggs to be cut' but 'the tenants should have wood or you will certainly be put to greater expense in the end'. Great care was taken to avoid waste. The steward reported regularly, writing 'John Baines and I have marked out timber in Upper Dalby Wood for Robert Boddy's Hay House. He tells me he will not be at any part of the expense of building it. It has two roomsteads in length 28 ft by 13, the expense of which will cost about £3 10s 0d. Tomorrow I begin to fall the wood at the Haggs and peel the bark. There will be about 500 feet fallen at Dalby and about 400 in the Haggs according to John Baines's estimation of them standing, but I shall be very particular in the admeasurement in both places, when the trees are fallen, of which you shall have an exact account, as also the quantity of bark sold from those trees'. His later report added 'as to the wood felled for Boddy's Hay House I had your orders lately that it should be built and accordingly John Baines set out wood as thought sufficiently for that building. Twenty-one trees may appear to you too much for that purpose but they were all very small and unimproveable, except one small tree of eight foot which was designed for a pair of forks that is to support the middle of the two roomsteads. But, in the workmanship of such crooked coarse timber, it must be observed great waist will be committed which cannot be avoided – and as to the expenses of felling and peeling, the bark will defray it'.

George Brown's house needed repair in 1748. The inside, the floors, plastering and window frames were 'almost destroyed by age'. Further afield, floods at Howe Ings below Pickering had washed away stoops and rails that needed replacement. Wood from Dalby was marked out for the butchers' shops at Pickering, probably the Market Place shambles. Timber was supplied to John Marshall altering his house in June 1746.

An account of the disposal of Dalby numbered timber being part of the number 750 set out by the commissioner in 1735 as follows, to wit - towards repairs of the tenants' houses.

Dalby	Tenant George Brown by John Baines	No	449	17ft	
		.	660	17ft	

In the year 1748 disposed of the numbered timber by John Wilson as follows

Dalby	Tenant Robert Boddy	518	13ft	7in
		683	9ft	
	Tenant George Brown	493	13ft	
			9ft	
		653	17ft	2in

In the year 1749

Dalby	Tenant George Brown	565	6ft	8in
		559	11ft	3in
		718	14ft	9in
		566	4ft	3in

In the year 1750

Dalby	Tenant Robert Boddy	577	10ft	2in
		547	18ft	9in
		458	15ft	3in

In the year 1742

Dalby		461	17ft	
		530	16ft	4in
		22	11ft	7in
		606	13ft	
		615	8ft	6in

Despite the bouyant demand for timber, high transport costs tended to keep its use local. Steward Wilmott, busily engaged in reconstructing Thornton Hall in 1748, wrote that 'the distance of leading the wood will amount at least £5 more than expected; the difference of the workmanship of that large wood for sawing etc will amount to at least £4 more'. This would add £9 to the cost over and above what it might have been if they had secured properly-sized trees from Haugh, making the total cost £29 instead of £20 (excluding what might be made from bark and firewood). Wood sold today might be needed tomorrow but the wealth of the estate owner enabled a long view to be taken. When a batch of six Dalby trees was cut, the 41 pieces were not sold but kept in George Brown's barn and at the bottom of the wood for future repairs of the premises. Oxen, 4-6 in a yoke were used for haulage. They could stand for long hours, soon fill their bellies in a pasture and were a good sheet anchor in a stiff uphill pull.

Small wood still went for a wider variety of uses. John Wilson spent five days at the haggs in 1746 felling wood for stoops and rails and then making them. Wilmot wrote in June 'as to the wood fallen at Dalby and the haggs'. Some had gone to 'repairs, plow and cart boot for Scalby' and 'also some gates, and in small repairs for the tenants at Thornton'. He observed that the tenants at Scalby would buy elsewhere 'rather than fetch if they have not timber worth fetching for plow and cart boot'. Oak went to board Richard Smales' barn floor in March 1749. The steward then looked at the oak and ash wood in Marshall's Ellerburn warren, for stoops and rails. He estimated 9 foot of timber for every twenty stoops and rails. He planned to take 1260 rails at 2940 foot and 420 stoops at 760 foot. There were too few ash, but a few were substantial and it 'would be a pity to use them all'. Some ordinary oaks there would do. As a compromise he tried to replace three rails deep by two and by winding them with thorns. Wood was cut before the sap had risen but he put off cutting the oaks till May, the time of bark peeling. He added, 'I think 2s apiece for the oak trees in the warren is higher than they would sell for excepting the bark'. In the end he thinned, leaving those 'proper to stand', used some ash, and looked in Old Dale for the rest that were needed.

Coppice wood had proved well suited to supporting a leather tanning industry and Thornton Dale had a large tannery. Robert Marshall pulled bark at the haggs in 1742 worth £6 15s. Barking was done late April and May though some thought oak peeled best in May and June. The steward wrote on the 29th April 1748 that 'it will not be long before the Dalby bark is ready to peel if the weather is constant'. Day labourers were employed for barking by the estate. Tanners working by the tun or quarter were thought not to peel close enough whereas labourers would peel small twigs down to finger thickness if the bark ran freely. It came off poles easily. It was dressed, stood against poles laid on forked stakes, or in wet weather laid along a bank of top wood, a foot off the ground, to dry off. It was chopped after delivery to the tanner. Income from bark for the steeping pits made some felling viable. Most bark from Dalby probably went to Thornton Dale, where John Priestman ran the tannery c1779, rebuilt it 1814, and saw his bark mill burnt down in 1849. The family sold the tannery to J R Hill in 1882.

Whether the Hills ever undertook any systematic planting at Dalby is not known. Sheep were great trespassers on the warrens in 1746 and later moved freely over much of their land. Both sheep and rabbits gnawed bark in severe winters and trees would die when it had gone from the lower trunk. By 1777 only a few stream side trees remained, a little hedgerow timber and small clusters at the lower parts of Flaxdale, Littledale and in Staindale east of the beck. West of the beck the haggs were still wooded. Later maps suggest fresh planting in the north-west of Dalby and further north within Lockton township. A shelterbelt was planted along the Cross Dyke between Kingthorpe and Lockton by 1821. South of Dalby, inclosure of commons fostered new planting by the Hills who also emparked Thornton Hall. Ellerburn Wood was planted on bare hillside in 1797 and in 1805 Cow Pasture

Bank and Duddy Hill were planted with young oaks, larches and Scots firs. Richard Hill paid John Storr £176 13s 9d in six payments for planting 32 acres and 20 perches of forest trees on Farmanby common at £5 10s an acre, completing in June 1810. Inclosure also made the landscape appear wooded outside plantations by encouraging the growth of miles of hedgerows. Shelterbelts spread, as farmsteads moved onto old commons. Planting ceased to be a novelty and improvers like John Tuke in 1794 were already aware that drained moor could support Scotch Fir and Norway spruce.

THE NEW GAME PRESERVES

The old forest laws had given way to general game laws in the Pickering district in the latter part of the 17th century. The old Statute of 1389 had protected 'gentlemen's game' from laymen with less than 40s a year in land and priests with less than £10 income a year. While minor game was plentiful, this probably had little effect upon the ordinary person seeking a small bird for the pot from the open commons by snare or trap. Loss of the old forest reduced some wild life but encouraged other birds and animals. Yet the property qualification for taking game was gradually raised until it became the privilege of only the larger landowners. The disappearance of the forest deer encouraged this, for the class who had enjoyed privileges in the forest turned to a new sport. All free-holders of under a hundred pounds, which meant the majority, were prohibited from killing game even on their own land in 1671. If the qualification for an 'estate of inheritance' was £100 per annum, that for leaseholders required life possession or a lease for 90 years or upwards, worth £150 a year. In the 18th century other restrictions were imposed and it was made illegal for most people to buy and sell game. This had the effect of raising the price that might be obtained for it by poachers.

During the 17th century, shooting had taken the place of hawking among the gentry. After c1690 the shooting of flying birds became popular. One result was that game was more rapidly destroyed. The rate of firing was increased by the introduction of the double-barrelled gun of the side-by-side type c1750 and by the improvements in guns resulting from the invention of Nock's Patent Breech in c1780. The rising quality of shooting as a sport attracted more gentry to it and killed more birds. Perhaps for the first time, for many birds, preservation became important to maintain the sport. One result was a spate of legislation known collectively as the Game Laws. From 1734 local gamekeepers were appointed for the larger local estates. Until then, Squire Hill had paid various local people for birds occasionally taken. In that year, his household accounts include payments of 2d for a snipe, 4d for a teal or partridge, 6d for a woodcock, or a pair of hares, and 1s for a pheasant. As late as October 1742 he paid R. Barker 2s for four moorgame. Yet, in 1734 he appointed James Wilson of Ruswarp as his gamekeeper for Pickering and Goathland and two years later made William Beilby keeper for Pickering Manor and Liberty. These served the Duchy estates. In 1740 he added

Roger Coates as gamekeeper for Thornton and Farmanby. Richard Barker followed, coming from Hill's Normanby and Welburn estates in 1744 and then George Brown of Dalby was given the job in October 1749.

An old saying states that 'to kill vermin is to breed game'. Keepers waged war on the enemies of the pheasant, partridge and hare. Since the rabbit shared the same enemies to a large extent, the keeper was also protecting the warrens. Gamekeepers were themselves allowed to kill game for the use of their employer. They also had power to seize guns, greyhounds, setting and other dogs, ferrets, snares and 'engines' for 'taking, killing and destroying of hares, pheasant, partridges and other game'. Sometimes a poacher found ways of getting his own back. When John Hill's steward approached the freeholders for their votes c1743 he had to report that 'Marshall, a notorious poacher of hares and rabbits, says he cannot be with us because your servant formerly took an old gun off him'. Silent bows, traps and nets were the poacher's more usual tools. Later in the century, inclosures increased the holdings of the large estates and reduced the area over which game could be taken most easily. Food scarcity among growing village populations during the Napoleonic Wars nonetheless fostered poaching. Gang poaching was sometimes organised to supply the high priced market and night poachers caught with nets became liable to transportation for seven years. The right of a tenant to interfere with an owner shooting his land was denied. In some places a state of war prevailed between keepers and poachers.

Hill's gamekeepers enjoyed some success at improving the estate as a game preserve. The house was well supplied and gifts sent to friends. Some 23 moorgame and 21 partridge went to the Archbishop of York in August 1743. After inclosure of nearby moors, when cultivation began to creep higher up the slope, many birds flourished on the increased crops. Even the red grouse, locally the 'moorcock', which avoided the farmed area and preferred the heather on a quick-drying surface, still found congenial conditions in north-east Yorkshire. Moors were managed to encourage them and corn put out for them in hard weather. The names Moorcock Inn, Moorbird Inn and Cockmoor witness one role of the land near the scarp in the early 19th century. Genteel shooting parties became a fashionable way of spending leisure. A famous old print shows Lord Middleton's party seeking grouse in nearby Newton Dale about 1790. From 1808, Mr Richard Hill became 'a keen preserver of partridges'. The 'nut brown birds' liked the cover of the newly inclosed field stubble but could suffer badly from vermin. Squire Osbaldeston wrote of 'shooting with my neighbour Richard Hill of Thornton, on his ground', boasting 'I killed 20 brace of partridge at 40 shots, never missing one. I did this with a flint and steel of 18 bore made by the celebrated Joe Manton'.

Burning off moors to give an annual supply of young heather fostered the grouse. Judging by the results of shoots, numbers increased through the 19th century with peaks in the 1870s. Keeper and huntsman John Booth who followed George Brown of Dalby from 1797 to 1853 saw some good years. After him c1863, Tom Cockerill was gamekeeper and then, in the halcyon years, the autocratic John Brewster. He was followed by James Green c1900 and George Craig c1926. The Reverend J R Hill, who used to call poachers 'pilgrims of the night', saw his estate much troubled between 1879 and 1882 by railway navvies who made night raids on his woods and warrens defended by under-keepers George Pickering of Ellerburn and John Smithies. In 1880 there was a battle with the poachers near Thornton Dale and a famous capture came when Mr Brewster took poachers with nets in Howldale in 1894. As well as warding off those not allowed to shoot, the keepers assisted in great guests' shoots when hundreds of birds might be knocked down in a day. Walking had begun to be superseded by driving in Yorkshire c1805 and became general in the 1840s. The old birds came over the gun first while the young flew a little way and settled again, so entire broods were not destroyed. Later, shoots had to be limited to sustain stocks of game.

Close preservation of game continued till the Ground Game Act of 1880 acknowledged the interests of the tenant-occupier. Ordinary people were less affected but the farmer was removed from the poacher's fraternity. Farm workers would set rabbit snares on their paths along a hedge side on the way to work and pick them up going home. More serious poachers sought partridges with long and purse nets. Gamekeepers would put brambles out to tangle them and had an armoury of other devices from tripwires and pitfalls to dummy pheasants. The gamekeepers were viewed as great men of the district. James Green had remarkable eyesight and could see movement in a hedge bottom hundreds of yards away. His rebuke to a gent who fired too quickly was 'birds are nea wuss'. When another missed a hare, he said 'aim sorry, aur aiam, for ai haven't a bigger un i parish'.

THE NEW HUNT

If a love of shooting was one criterion of the new 'gentleman', a fondness for horses, hounds and hunting was another. A Sinnington pack already hunted the district but John Hill formed his own pack of foxhounds in Queen Anne's time. His relative Sir William Hustler of Acklam Hall in Cleveland offered him an 'extra-ordinary well bred whelp' in 1713-14, arguing that it was too large and too fast for the pack he was raising from the eight couple of dogs he had bought. He recalled that Hill has said to him at Thornton that he liked his dogs to go 'as fleet as he could get them'.

There is a tradition that a later squire, Mr Richard Hill, or possibly one of his forebears, hunted carted deer at Thornton. It is not likely to date back to John Hill's time, for the mention in his household accounts of sending berries and venison to Scarborough in August 1735, is followed a month later by a note that he had bought a haunch from Lord Carlisle's gamekeeper and the deer were probably on the Castle Howard estate. Mr R J Hill may have had a pack of stag hounds. Kennels in the grounds, a box for deer and a deer-cart were remembered after his day and perhaps account for Dog Kennel Lane in Thornton. Richard Hill was a field sportsman and kept a few couple of beagles at home, while attending Oxford in his teens. In 1808, the year that he came of age, he refounded the Derwent Pack. They were often seen at Dalby. Using his own stock and some crosses with Sir Tatton Sykes' Wold Pack, he bred 'for nose and music' which he thought essential in a hard and sometimes impassable country. John Booth served him as both gamekeeper and huntsman. By 1820 there was a valuable pack but they were stricken by hydrophobia in 1831-2 when he lost twelve couple of hounds and other dogs. When Booth died after 56 years service, and at the age of 85, during 1853, the Squire placed a memorial inscribed 'Well done, good and faithful servant'.

Jack Hill kept the pack going until 1862. His foxhounds were in Dalby on New Year's Day 1856, and on many another occasion. Some foxes came easily but others would beat the pack unless hard-pressed for half an hour or more during the run. There were good and bad scent days. Control of the hounds belonged with the huntsman and his whippers-in. With the popularity of 'hunting to ride' as against 'riding to hunt', horse-control and knowing how to put him to every kind of fence became a considerable skill. Farmers whose ewes slipped lambs, or who saw crops damaged, could do little about it until a later age. Strips of noses from foxes taken went to ornament the Thornton Hall stable doors. Old Willie Ecclefield (1794-1872) was kennel man and hound-keeper. He played flute in church and once cooked a fox and ate it to see what it tasted like. After the pack was sold, it ceased to be kennelled at Thornton Dale, but the Derwent may still be seen there.

INCLOSURE OF THE COMMONS

Dalby had never had commons since Norman times but its neighbours were well endowed and early inclosure had barely encroached upon them. The land that would have been commons had Dalby's earlier history been different became rabbit warren. The end of the neighbouring commons came as part of the movement to inclose by Act of Parliament at the end of the 18th century. Until this time, Dalby stood out as a 'ancient enclosure' bounded north by the beck and other ancient enclosures beyond it in Staindale, bounded west by Lockton South Moor and Pexton Moor, bounded east by Thornton Common, Allerston Low Moor and some small Allerston inclosures in south Staindale, and bounded south by Thornton and Farmanby Commons, of which part had been brought into Flainsey Warren. Their areas were vast: Ellerburn Common (600 acres), Kingthorpe (364 acres), Thornton and Farmanby (691 acres), Lockton South Common (1142 acres) as late as 1795.

The Inclosure movement changed much else. Where piecemeal inclosure had not already exchanged small individually owned fields for the common arable fields, it completed that process. On the moors, except for marginal land well to the north, common rights were given up and inclosed plots of land awarded in their place. Dalby lost its distinctiveness in the landscape, as in the years that followed, new boundary hedges and walls for small fields were pushed northwards where the commons had been. So much land went to the manor owner at Allerston that its ring-fence estate showed little immediate change but the other neighbours saw their landscape transformed. Several owners of messuages, cottages, tofts and frontsteads claiming common rights on Flainsey Rigg secured compensation at the hearings preceding the 1780 inclosure of Thornton Dale east of the beck. The Act of Parliament of 1777 had provided that one sixtieth of the 800 acre common should go to the Crown. Under the 1795 inclosure of Farmanby, Ellerburn and Kingthorpe, the Dean and Canons of Windsor received an award of 168 acres against Dalby wood. The commons as well as the West, Middle and East Fields of Allerston were inclosed 1805-10 and Squire Osbaldeston made a training gallop on Allerston Moor soon after. Under the different awards, the Duchy, and hence their lessors, received awards close to land already held, including 47 acres 3 roods 1 perch west of Dalby Hagg in Lockton South Moor and 123 acres 2 roods 2 perch in Allerston.

Inclosure commissioners specified the dimensions of dry stone walls to be raised at Lockton, where live hedges were hard to raise. Relatively cheap and durable, they had to be at least 5ft high with a coping. The alternative was ditches 2ft 6in wide at the top and 18in deep with a quickset planted 12in away. Local walls were made double or single, often with a 22in base and 15in crest, coped against the sheep. Using a wood frame as a guide, a man could make seven yards for 5s 6d using three cartloads of stone to the yard. Some had a 34in base of large flat stones, then at 30in up a row of through stones, and at the top double 18in stone laid across. Each stone had to rest on two others while spaces were firmly packed with small stones. The Victorians sometimes placed coping stones projecting a couple of inches and bedded in lime. A well-made dry stone wall would withstand all weathers. For hedging, whitethorn or quickwood was much in demand and usually planted when three years old. More boundaries meant more gates of the local variety – a five bar gate with bars of fir or ash and a harltree or head of oak. The gateposts were often massive stones. Inside the new closes, paring, burning and liming was the method of improving the old wastes. The paring spade broke up the coarse rough turf. The lime produced sweeter herbage. Turfs were burnt on their edge after drying, the ashes spread by women as a manure and ploughed in.

The commissioners laid out many miles of new roads to give access to new fields. Older routes faded out or dwindled to the status of footpaths. New roads were declared to be king's highways and hence 'common and public carriage roads' or private roads, in which case the users to whom they were private were specified.

Dalby as an ancient inclosure was untouched by such revisions. At Lockton the 1784 Act and 1795 Award laid down a public carriage road, called the Overscarr Road, running east from the Whitby-Pickering road, along which stagecoaches were now travelling. It left it near the corner of Lockton's Brim Field, going over the Overscarr Quarry, 40ft wide to Dalby Hagg. The Lyddygate Road in Lockton was declared a private road, to run 27ft broad from a point near Breck Nook east over South Moor to a gate called Lyddygate at the entrance to Dalby Hagg. It was for the use of the king's tenants and for all others going to Dalby. The faint dotted line on the Dalby map of 1777 marks its continuation, coinciding with the Lidygate Way on early Ordnance Survey maps.

The Allerston Act of 1800-1 and the Award of 1818 laid down a public carriage road or highway, 40ft wide, called the Kingthorpe and Hackness Road, leading from Scamridge in Ebberston to the north-east corner of Dalby Warren. It entered Thornton Common at the Wetmoor Dyke. The Thornton Dale Award names a public carriage road or king's highway, of breadth 40ft called the Thornton and Ellerburn Road, to run from Whitbygate via Kirkdale to Ellerburn. It replaced an earlier Thornton-Ellerburn Road on a different alignment.

THE YEARS OF IMPROVED FARMING

After inclosure had become general through the district, Dalby farms lost much of their distinctiveness. No record has yet come to light to show the type of farming adopted in early Victorian times but it probably shared much with comparable dales, the main difference being the continued working of the rabbit warrens. Despite these, the high ground of Stoneclose Rigg, Newclose Rigg and later Adderstone Rigg and Clenfield Rigg saw enclosures made and some attempt to improve the pasture. In nearby Allerston Moor, the sites of 14th century sheep folds were inclosed by the late 18th century, and a farmhouse or Warren House for Staindale Warren was built before 1830. Jingleby Hall was built not long after. Within Dalby, Riggs Farm was eventually sited near the largest enclosure on Stoneclose Rigg but at a rather later date. Once founded, its clearances expanded to take up most of the rigg and overlapped onto others. Its arable fields contain old quarries for lime and limekilns used to prepare field dressing. On the other side of the valley, Thornton Common House was built on Pexton Moor amid its new fields.

Township boundaries lost much of their importance after inclosure, for at the same time church tithes were replaced by money rents or awards of land. Until 1777 the Thornton Dale rector had drawn tithes in kind from two of the Dalby farms, probably for land east of the beck, while Ellerburn Church had received tithes of the Ings west of the beck. In the whole Thornton Parish the rector had received one tenth of all corn and hay grown east of the beck, the tenth fleece of wool at shearing time, tithe lambs on St Peter's Day, tithe calves, foals, geese, ducks, turkeys, and pigs, paid when they were three years old. He had a penny from each swarm of bees and a tenth of honey and wax from old stock. Tithes were in kind for a sewn crop but money was paid if a field was in grass. Each house paid a hen at St Thomas's Day. Instead of these dues, he was awarded $2/15^{th}$ of the field land and $1/10^{th}$ of the commons.

The Duchy of Lancaster estate boundaries expanded to take in awarded land, which was let along with that at Dalby. The Hill family continued to tenant the Duchy estate, despite a severe blow when the squire lost £28500 guineas in play with Mr Barry. The debt was settled at £5000 in 1792, about the same time that the squire was only just deterred from staking his manor on a game of billiards with the older George Osbaldeston. Not surprisingly, at his death in the next year, R J Hill left a burdened estate, and his heirs within two years had to borrow £1000 on a mortgage of the Dalby farms. By 1853 Low Dalby tenants were holding much land at Thornton as well as in Dalby. The large farm holding embraced 2294 acres one rood 16 perches and paid a rent of £625 7s 2d. Of the old grounds it included Longlands Close, Crofts Below Wood, High, Low, Great and Highgate Ings, High and Low Wood Warren, Low Warren, half of Turf Moor and Keld House Garth, but it also included the north part of Ellerburn Warren, Pexton Moor, Whitecliff Rigg, Flainsey Rigg, and around Thornton Dale, Wood Close, Harrow Cliffs, Wandales, High, Middle and Low Hurrell and Harland's Closes. The Hills had finally bought out the Dean and Chapter of Windsor's interests in 1869, giving them great flexibility in managing their estate. The rabbit types were spread further afield on newly enclosed land at Pexton Moor.

High Dalby Farm still stood open to the sward but new farm buildings, built a little north-east at the low end of the well-trodden Little Dale, gave a good fold yard. Burnt lime was used instead of old earth mortar, and chiselled freestone from the calcareous grit for quoins combined with the more easily worked limestone, hammered on one face. Slate and pantile replaced limestone tiles and thatch. Low Dalby gained a more scattered cluster of buildings including a row of good stables. Rigg Farm was given two blocks forming the north and east sides of a square. An old building at Upper Swairdale in 1777 disappeared and Sibdale End House seems early to have gone to ruin. Further down the valley a Nabgate House was built on old Thornton Commons east of the beck while High Paper Mill came to be called Musdale House, and had its own Musdale sandstone quarry nearby. The mill buildings show features of several dates but the mill is apart from the roadside house, standing athwart a narrow race with no obvious source of water above ground. Further north is a waterfall diverting to Paper Mill Pond, known as High Fish Pond in 1850. It is said to have been built as a settling or filtering bed by Richard Hill after dye had poisoned trout. Sand was used to clean the water source behind. The arch of a wheelpit is visible in the building near the stream.

Buildings at the old Hermit Close seem to have fallen to ruin in the 18th century. Some rebuilding was attempted in 1735 when the estate steward wrote in January 'I have not yet obtained a perfect information of James Boyes house, but shall be industrious in finding it out as soon as I can. But in such an affair, I apprehend I must be cautious of whom I inquire for particulars thereof, or anything else concerning him. As to stones, he has not made use of any fresh ones but such as came out of the old frontstead, such he has applied to this new house'. Mr Hill seems to have acquired the copyhold in c1744. In 1748, we hear that 'John Boyes Close which is called by the name of Keldhousegarth has hitherto been used as meadow ground being a piece improper for any other purpose since it is very full of bogs and springy kind of land. It adjoins south of Brown's Low Wood and Ing with which it was sometimes let'. The Reverend John Webb in 1795 claimed exception from all tithes for Keldhouse Garths otherwise Skeller Garths, he paying 3s a year to the vicar of Ellerburn instead. Skeller Garths were further towards Ellerburn, west of the stream, but they may once have had some link with the Hermitage Close. Skewthwaite or Ellers Wood is mentioned in 1436. In 1850 and in 1976 a small unimpressive square of building stood in Keldhousegarth; it was puzzlingly described as Harwood House. The only known Harwood connected with the area was John Harwood, servant of Sir Roger Hastings, who was rescued by him one night from Pickering Castle prison in 1498.

Traffic from the Crosscliffe and Staindale farms and others of the new moor-edge sometimes came down through Dalby. Some roads gained a rough limestone surface unfriendly to the ox which consequently vanished from the roads. Most roads were still soaked and cut up in winter, the wagon ruts stiffening in the winds of March but soft again to the hoof in summer. The road over Stoneclose Rigg was straightened between 1777 and 1857 to go between new inclosures. Replacement of an old building east of High Dalby allowed some diversion there. Fords across the beck gained wooden footbridges. Near Jingleby the Moorbird Inn, with its own stableman and wheelwright, ran through much of the century. It is now ruined. West of Dalby the Keld House built at another crossing on Lockton's South Moor before 1821 was by 1840 converted into a beer house called the Fox and Rabbit. It still serves as a meeting place for shepherds, sportsmen, travellers and farmers. The gamekeeper ran the Allerston Inn in 1810 and Lockton had its own Durham Ox Inn. Thornton Dale had the New Inn, the Buck and four beer houses in 1840.

Late 19th century maps show Dalby's woodland largely confined to Haygate Wood, Low Wood and High Wood, some streamside trees in Dalby and Staindale, and an orchard at Low Dalby but Flaxdale bottom was now clear. The Holm Woods in High Staindale and Ellers Wood in Ellerburn still carried evergreen cover. Wilton Heights and Black Plantation Crossdike contained mixed plantings but Pexton Moor, Warren and Black House Plantations, Allerston were mainly conifers. The latter were sufficient to supply the sawmill set up at Allerston in c1847.

It is doubtful if the rabbit warrens were kept up on the old scale. By 1850, wild rabbits were increasingly numerous, spreading out from the warrens and occupying hedgerow burrows. Farmers came to view them much as they saw the rat, as a threat to their livelihood. Lurcher dogs were kept and traps set a-plenty long before the law recognised the need. A letter of 1937, from the tenant at Low Kingthorpe to his landlord reveals the scope of the problem.

'Dear Mr Wheldon

I am sorry to have to write you this letter, but I am going to state in this letter what is right and what I intend to do, as I cannot possibly pay any rent on a farm like this and pay wages as I will soon lose every penny I have. The rabbits are eating everything that grows. It is most shameful. I have 36 loads of corn sown and I will do well if I get 3 or 4 loads from the whole lot, there is only the barley field near the house that is good, the wheat they ate it all off and the oats too. So what my horses will live on in winter I am at loss to know.'

He proposed to sell his stock and 'clear out'.

Back in the 19th century, Richard Hill's printed tenancy agreements with his farmers had offered few legal options for dealing with game and to a point had controlled farming procedure. Clauses required them

- Not to plough or sow arable, except in a due and regular course of husbandry.
- Not to take more than 2 crops of corn or grass successively, but to summer fallow or fallow with turnips, to be eaten upon the ground by sheep.
- Not to take two crops in immediate succession on light lands, adapted to seed and turnip husbandry, but to sow their first crop of corn after turnips, with a sufficient quantity of good grass seed, to one, two or three years at his or their discretion and then be ploughed again and sown with wheat or oats.
- To lay and spread yearly on every acre of fallow or turnip land, not less than 3 caldrons of well burnt lime, or 12 cartloads of good rotten manure.
- To at all times lay the whole of the manure bred upon the premises upon the turnip-fallowed lands and upon the meadow and pasture lands.
- Not to remove any hay, straw, manure, dung or compost from the farm but cause it to be consumed there.
- Not to plant more than a stated quantity of acres of potatoes in any year.
- Not to fell, lop or top any trees, or buckhead, or remove any thorns.
- To preserve all quickwood and keep it guarded, cleared and weeded.
- Not to kill or destroy or permit to be killed or destroyed any game, but to preserve and encourage the breed for the use of Richard Hill 'whose gamekeepers as well as himself and any other persons in his company or having his leave, shall have free liberty to hunt for and kill the same'.

Tenants at Low Dalby were George Brown (1756-8), Robert and Anne Champley (1780-1812), Thomas Cross (1824), Gessle Poad Robinson (1834), Thomas Cross senior and John Cross (1843), John Cross (1869), and Mrs Rachel Cross (1872). Brown was a church warden down the valley at Ellerburn and Champley left a great tomb in the Thornton churchyard.

James Green, gamekeeper, Thornton Dale, 1928, in a derelict rabbit trap or 'type'.
This was sunk in the ground with a tip-board which dropped the rabbit into the
stone-lined trap. Several dozen rabbits could be caught in one night.
[Ryedale Folk Museum]

5

DALBY – FROM FARMING TO FOREST

The challenge to British farming from railway- and steamship-borne crops and meat from overseas producing countries during the later 19th century transformed the prospects of countryside places like Dalby. Though there was a boom during the 1914-19 World War, hard years came again until a second World War brought a renewed concern with increasing national farm production. Though dales farms had changed more slowly than many others, their great days were over. Innovation long ceased as the years of Victorian capital investment in the landscape gave way to 'make and mend'. Farm workers left the countryside in a steady flow. Victorian methods continued in a deteriorating landscape as hedges, ditches and walls lost the lavish 'cheap labour' maintenance they had earlier enjoyed. After 1880 land that had been cleared during the enclosure movement was frequently to be found reverting to rough grazing. Bracken spread and the wasteland reappeared.

The Population of Thornton, with Ellerburn and Farmanby, Parishes

Stage of growth				Stage when static			Stage of decline			
1801	1811	1821	1831	1841	1851	1861	1871	1881	1891	1901
1227	1380	1485	1560	1572	1581	1541	1439	1426	1267	1163

By 1901, the Parish population was below that of 1801.

The running down of the old way of life was gradual and such trends are rarely well recorded. Tenant farmers adapted to changes as best they could. Old John Boddy was the last of that family at High Dalby where he farmed from 1866 to 1886. He is said to have been followed by a Mr Hoggard but on other accounts the Brewster family were there from 1887 to 1918. Mr Brewster of Levisham, who went there at the age of three, remembered horse-drawn vehicles from Burgess's Mill at Thornton Dale and funeral parties, with a wagon used as the hearse, making their way across High Dalby and up by Riggs to Givendale. Frank Burgess farmed High Dalby from 1918 to 1920, possibly being followed by the Boyes family. The record for Low Dalby is less complete. Old John Cross died there in 1869. Lawrence Jackson farmed it in the early 20th century and Frank Avison in c1921.

The old industries down the valley were abandoned as manufacture became concentrated in the great industrial areas. The Thornton Dale tannery closed and both the paper and bleach mills at Ellerburn were converted into small farms. The old industrial buildings were adapted as sheds and stores or simply fell down. The remains of races, ponds and mills form an intriguing monument of 'industrial archaeology'. The rabbit warrens were no longer maintained in the old 'model' manner. The types fell in but catchers continued to be employed as the rabbits were now virtually out of control. Mr Dowson of Marishes was one of the last catchers of the old school.

One woodland industry to survive well into the 20th century was 'clogging'. Up to the first world war, John Raw would work his way up the valley cutting alder logs, which stood piled high to dry in his garden. He made the clog soles, hard but surprisingly pliable, which many local people wore. There were Sunday and weekday clogs, stuffed with straw by farm workers to make them more comfortable. Many were sent away by rail for the mills of Lancashire. Hazel rods were also gathered to make hurdles within living memory, some being debarked by laying them out in the enclosures near some of the old rabbit types, for the rabbits to nibble on.

Thornton Dale kept its mill and would ultimately develop large quarries but its social structure changed. The Hill family left the Hall, which was converted into a hotel. As far back as 1903-10 there was a spate of villa building. It had already become a place to retire to and after being voted the prettiest village in Yorkshire in 1907 it began to attract more tourist visitors. At first they came by rail and stayed a week or two in villa and cottage homes but excursions from Scarborough brought early trippers as well. A few found their way up to the beauty spot at Dalby Griff. Children on Sunday school treats enjoyed the valley.

The farms at Dalby had never been quite as isolated as their situation suggests. For centuries, they had been producing the equivalent of a 'cash-crop'. The widening of markets for farm produce altered their relative self-sufficiency less than the general rise in living standards. More of what was bought for farm use and the larder came from distant places. Socially, Dalby had always looked to the churches and villages down the valley. Methodism enriched dale life with cottage meetings and provided, for a time, small chapels at Lockton and Saltersgate. Thornton Dale and Lockton had a rich social life with Wesleyan and Primitive Methodist societies, well-stocked shops, smithies and other craft workshops, friendly societies and clubs. Sunday school and chapel anniversaries and club feasts were high points of the year. Thornton's quadrille band was launched in 1866 and its brass band ten years later while at Ellerburn Church Thomas Widd's cello gave way to a new harmonium in c1910.

'Gentry farming', by someone not totally dependent on the land for income, could still reverse the trend, if only with difficulty. The Coulson family came to High Dalby in c 1923-4. An elder son, Arthur Tranmer Coulson came first but in 1924-5 his father John Arthur Coulson, his sons and daughters all moved in and Tranmer moved to farm elsewhere. Born at Langton Grange, John had enjoyed a 25 year lease at Watton Priory. Something of a gentleman farmer, he had yet acquired some engineering training. He was well travelled, making visits to Russia and New Zealand when such trips were rare. He liked to experiment in many fields and with Frank Butler of Scarborough was a founder member of 'Malton Fertilisers' later the Malton Farmers' Manure Company.

High Dalby gained many innovations. To accommodate his 16hp 1922-3 Cubitt open tourer car he metalled the road at a cost reputed to be several hundred pounds. The road north to Rose Cottage was already semi-metalled but a German named Lindhart who lived there and owned the fishing did not like people on his land. Five acres was fenced off near the High Dalby house and given a rockery and a ton of daffodil and narcissus bulbs, whose progeny in later years spread down the valley. An extension was put on the house rear and a conservatory on the front. Blacksmith Willie Dalton, who had shod his home-bred shire horses, came over from Watton to build a self-shutting oak gate which would close without effort either way. A bridge was made across the stream using old Bradford tram lines for girders.

The farm foreman, a Mr Warrener, lived at Rigg Cottage on the high ground, a character 'solid as a rock'. A 'shocking road' led there but Coulson installed the Dutch barn. Walter Greenheld walked down from Lockton daily to work at High Dalby where Mr Dickinson, his wife and daughter Betty 'lived in'. They kept three or four hundred sheep and most of the land was grazing. The 40 acre field near Riggs was ploughed and some more above the west side, but as an experiment a hundred acres of moor near Riggs was cleared of bracken, ploughed and sown with oats, possibly in conjunction with Leeds University. The result was patchy and it returned to pasture. Horses were used for ploughing till a large International tractor was bought. A couple of hundred head of poultry, a few pigs and some cows for milk made up the stock.

Much of what was needed came from the farm. They baked their own bread on the big kitchen range. John Coulson made a walled kitchen garden and planted a sizeable orchard that gave fair plums, cherries and apples, used for eating, bottling and jams. Blackcurrants were plentiful. There was a vine as well as a heliotrope in the conservatory. Exotics in the garden included a medlar tree and a green rose from Watton that he named 'Bertha Coulson'. Hams were cured, after killing the pigs outside the blacksmith's shop with an iron punch. John experimented with edible fungi but failed to rouse his family's enthusiasm. They preferred the mushrooms that grew in Sneverdale. The lads would take their air rifle to shoot at the rookery on the west side or in Sneverdale and their shoot went for rook pie. One lad remembers his brother bringing a carrion crow egg down from a tree top carried in his mouth. The fishing rights ran up into Staindale and to Low Dalby, several miles that supplied brown trout. The father taught the boys to cast flies onto a postcard on his tennis green.

Rabbits came easily and could be caught by the score. One year, 998 couple were sold, weighing seven pounds the couple. They sold at 11d to 1s a pair in 1932-3, the best year. Walter Greenheld did the snaring but one of the sons, John Aymar Coulson, remembers shooting them, 12 or 14 in an evening, from the stone wall against the 70 acre field at Riggs Farm. His father designed a rabbit carrier for Greenheld, pushed along with two wooden wheels; it could carry 50 or 60 couple. Snipe, woodcock and heron could be found and the occasional mallard. Just as the Thornton Dale historian Jeffrey enjoyed boyhood visits to Flaxdale Spring Foot, for nutting below the rookery and amidst primroses, so the Coulson boys found berries and nuts further up the valley.

On a farm with capital available, improvements came that would only become normal in the district after the Second World War, with subsidies and grants. The stone walls were kept up and posts and barbed wire used for fencing the higher ground. An acetylene gas plant with an 'up and down' cylinder went into a farm outbuilding. The stream was dammed and a small hydraulic ram raised water to a header tank in the farm roof, 'only just managing it'. It supplied two bathrooms, and washbasins in two or three bedrooms installed for guests. About 1935-6, as farming returns dropped, Coulson turned to taking paying guests. The farm buildings grouped around a stackyard to the east had a one-storey building one side, a two-storey structure on the other where wool was stored in sacks after shearing, and the blacksmith's shop with a grindstone outside nearer to the farm. When the old Cubitt car went off the road, it was put in the stackyard with a pulley on its propshaft to drive a circular saw. At least one son learned to change gear there.

The farm was much troubled by pests, including foxes. Traps were set for stoats and weasels. Moles moved through the tennis court. The farm dogs included a bull terrier called Tarzan, a black retriever known as Ben and a labrador who liked to sink in the stream bed and re-emerge carrying a sandstone. He chewed these so much he wore his teeth down to stubs. When forest planting began down the dale, the pests at first increased. Shooting was restricted, the Derwent hunt could not get in to the foxes, and 70 lambs could be lost in a year. The farmer felled his own trees as needed to make fence posts. The farm may have had its own sawpit. One felling method was to drill a small hole with an auger and put a small charge in. The felled trees were split with wedges.

Journeys were made once a week to Pickering market on Monday, or to Malton Co-operative Stores to get supplies. In place of the Cubitt, the farmer bought a Mathis from Holliday's Garage at Pickering and later a Wolseley. One of the lads roared about on a motorcycle. They stored some peat but coal came from the railhead at Pickering – 'Derby Brights' at 35s a ton, hauled back on a trailer. A haircut at the barber in the 'vaults' was 2d or 3d. Young John Coulson's first watch came from Crawford's in Burgate. Supplies were stocked up against winter when they might be cut off for a month. Once they cut through deep drifts to the Fox & Rabbit to get poultry feed and brought it back on a sled. Dr Murphy would call at the farm from Pickering, staying three hours for a game of chess and his tea.

J A Coulson, born in 1915, went to school at Terrington and Pocklington but returned to the dale for holidays and weekends. His older brothers and sisters moved away, Claude emigrating to East Africa in 1929. A sister Lois went in 1931-2 to open a tea room at Streatham. John joined the police in 1936 and served as an air force pilot 1941-6. Meanwhile the father was supplementing farming by involvement in the summer tourist trade. Shooting parties and anglers came, among them, in his old Daimler, Tim Holtby who fished with hooks. In a quarry up the dale was a clay pigeon machine for extra sport till it rusted away. In the cycling age visitors could get 'wonderful ham teas' for 1s at the Fox & Rabbit. Uninvited cars came sometimes into the dale only to be greeted by the farmer's notice on the gate which proclaimed 'Terras Aquilene running wild. Danger'. It referred to the bracken, but was effective.

Meanwhile, more dramatic changes were taking place in lower Dalby. The First World War had seen great felling of timber nationally and revealed the growing scarcity of this natural resource. Woods that the Cayley family, squires of Allerston, had planted north of that village were felled in 1916. They had cost £3 an acre to establish. Planting costs were now much higher but when the time came to commence post-war reconstruction, the creation of new timber reserves was given high priority. As a result, the Forestry Commission was set up by Act of Parliament in 1919, charged to create reserves of standing timber for the nation. Though it was empowered to assist private afforestation, it was clear that creating timber as a renewable resource needed longer term planning than one individual's life and more resources than could be supplied by the relatively hard-pressed owners of private estates. This decision brought the forest back to Dalby. Low density sheep grazing, rabbit warrens and game preserves would give way before trees.

THE FORESTRY COMMISSION'S FIRST PLANTATIONS

The Forestry Commission was formed in 1919 to grow timber, to assist private forests, to research forestry and to encourage forest industries. An essential first step was to acquire sites for planting, and possible areas in the North York Moors were viewed that year. Negotiations aimed at acquiring land continued during 1920 and on 3rd March 1921 a local grant of 1593 acres was made by the Duchy of Lancaster. On 23rd March, some 966 acres of the Allerston estate were bought from Sir Kenelm Cayley. The Dalby land acquired included the old estates that the Hill family had tenanted, with valley meadow and grazing ground but mostly high rough grazings where heather quickly became dominant. Some small part of the better oolite land was growing corn but rough grazing predominated. The old township of Dalby formed the larger part and gave name to Dalby Forest, though this included Allerston land and other acquisitions outside the old boundary.

First plantings were made in 1921. Some say these were on the riggs above Sandale at Dalby. Others claim the earliest were made above Allerston village. From the beginning, there were attempts to plough before planting but ordinary farm ploughs cut too shallow a furrow to be effective. Experience in planting moory land on upper slopes with diverse soils was only slowly built up. The whole project was a vast experiment. Its progress was hindered by government financial retrenchment in the face of a difficult national economic situation in 1922. Funds were cut and staff struggled to maintain planned programmes. From 1921 to 1927, an average of 440 planted acres a year was projected.

More land was steadily acquired for future use. It would form the nucleus of the later Wykeham, Langdale and Cropton forests. Some 1200 acres at Hutton Buscel Moor and Baker's Warren (Troutsdale) were leased from Lord Downe's Wykeham estate on 9th October 1924, and planting began at Baker's Warren two years later. A first purchase on the Crosscliffe estate, absorbed into Dalby Forest, was made in 1926. Some 1348 acres at Harwood Dale were leased from Lord Derwent in 1927 and the first lease made on the Keldy Castle estate near Cropton. The first plantings at Rosedale near Cropton, some 284 acres, were made in 1928.

Plantings topped 10000 acres for the first time in 1927 but grave doubts had emerged as to the success of earlier work. The experiment was barely succeeding. Plateau pines were growing very slowly and over 200 acres of spruce had 'gone into check'. The hard decision was taken to cut the local annual planting programme in 1928 to 150 acres. Meanwhile a research scheme was launched at Wykeham and Harwood Dale to discover more effective ways of establishing trees on the difficult and varied soils and terrains. Early attempts at ploughing before planting had been abandoned and most of the early plantations were established with the spade. Horse drawn agricultural ploughs were tried again in Dalby Forest during 1928 but they merely scratched the surface for the spade to follow.

The heath soils often covered a dry stony, acid iron pan, about one eighth of an inch thick and some nine to eighteen inches down, which effectively hindered root growth. Penetrating this was too much for the horse and beyond the plough. Outside the pan areas, ploughing or individual planting might be more successful but enormous weed growth and rapid recovery of heather hindered growth unless labourers, who might spend October making roads, and November to April planting, were fully engaged on weeding from June to September, at heavy cost. Other areas carried 'gley' soils which became waterlogged in winter, restricting root growth to their upper layers unless drained and cultivated beforehand. Yet other areas carried true peat. Much land was high, between the 400ft and 800ft contours, with heavy rainfall and exposed to wind and winter gales. Snow lingered longer than in Pickering Vale. Variations of slope, soil character and depth, aspect and 'mini-climate' presented highly different chances of success with different tree species. Bleak exposed land, sometimes very dry in summer and waterlogged in winter, was not by its nature immediately favourable to tree growth. It had to be made so.

Local reactions to the new forests were focused on less technical matters. Existing farms and good grazings were little disturbed as long as planting kept to the upper slopes and moors. Yet concentration on such land made the new woodlands highly visible. A writer of 1929 spoke for some, when he eulogised the browns, coppers and reds of autumn bracken and purple heather vanishing from his Thornton landscape before thousands of tiny conifers planted in straight rows. Heckdale and the warrens had been known for the diverse, parallel but sweeping lines of vegetation that followed the rocks and soils along the contours. Young plantings were unattractive. Their straight lines infuriated countryside romantics along with straight forest rides and streams forced into straight beds. A Thornton Dale man bemoaned the felling of the nutwood at Dalby and its replacement by larch and spoke of White Grass of Parnassus at the lower end of Sandale as if it was a treasure soon to be lost. Even the broody mass of mature forest held little appeal for those used to open moor and hardwood coppice.

Other critics objected to the idea of 'state forests', an image the Commission would only slowly lose, on political grounds. Since founding a national reserve of timber required investment on behalf of a future generation, the cash allocations for the purpose were all too easy a subject for the axe of economy. It was in 1931, when ploughing equipment partly adequate to meet the main technical difficulty was being devised, that the most severe financial cuts were made and planting programmes had to be savagely pruned. The situation recurred in the following year when the Oliver double furrow plough was actually being put into use at Dalby.

SOLVING THE PROBLEMS OF THE YOUNG FOREST

Adapting the land to take trees, selecting trees to suit the land and training unskilled workers in forestry techniques were the classic problems of the early years. The first plantings had to gain some maturity before the worst problems were realised. Some of them would never come to full fruition and left later foresters with a choice between clear felling or the long wait for the trees slowly to reach a more useful maturity. Others proved viable and would eventually provide good timber. The trees planted were mainly conifers which were broadly suited to the infertile moorland soils and would offer reasonably quick growth.

Autumn and early spring planting was done by gangs, each man carrying a bag of seedlings from his shoulder. In soft soil, young trees were 'notched' in with a spade, but hard, stony or rooted ground had to be loosened with a mattock and opened out to receive the roots. The ground was then firmly trod. It was done on piece work and a good man might plant 1200 in a day, spacing the seedlings about five feet each way, so making about 1700 trees to the acre, allowing for rides. Moor sheep had to be fenced or netted out, and fine mesh net was necessary if rabbits were to be excluded. Either would destroy the seedlings. 'Forest protectors' or 'warreners' were employed to keep down the rabbits. Weeds, scanty on old heather ground but prolific in old grass, bracken or woodland, would smother the young trees unless annually cut. From June to September, men and women weeded with sickles till the young trees rose above weed level.

First steps towards the more successful establishment of young trees came with the re-introduction of adapted horse-drawn farm ploughs at Black House in 1928. Four years later, the superior Oliver double furrow plough was introduced, at Dalby. Using a mouldboard, it gave two furrows, five foot apart for planting. An Oliver plough with a sub-soiler was also used for shallow ploughing at Cropton in 1934, and in the same year the first crawler tractor. A Caterpillar twenty was used to give motive power at Jingleby Thorn. A Killifer sub soiler was tried behind an Oliver plough at Dalby in 1938 but the arrangement proved cumbersome. Heavier ploughs, sub-soilers and tractors solved the worst problem by penetrating the compacted impervious 'pan' of washed down minerals that so often underlay the thin soil and thicker peat layers. Thirty years of experiment culminated in the decision made in 1942 to develop the first specialised forestry plough. After experiments by Lord Robinson, this was designed by the Commission's mechanical equipment officer, in conjunction with the agricultural machinery firm of Russell's of Kirkbymoorside. It was called the RLR plough.

The RLR at last effectively broke into the iron pan, typical of at least 35% of the Commission's local land. It cut a deep furrow of about 18 inches and effectively suppressed the heather for some years in its wake. People began to speak of 'prairie-busters'. During the later war years the early farm tractors were replaced by such heavy duty machines as the Fowler 'Coffee Pot' Field Marshall machine of 55 horse power. During the 1950s a second generation of ploughs were designed.

One of the most important was the Parkgate tine plough, which had a share elongated to act as a strong sub-soiling tine. The tine broke the pan within its reach. A deep furrow was cut and the upturned slice of soil was turned over onto the heather. The Cuthbertson draining plough was adapted for the peat lands where it overturned the turf so that spruce roots could be set shallow beneath.

RLR plough [M Laurie, Forestry Commission]

Ploughing remained impossible in really rocky ground and in old woodland new trees were planted among old stumps by hand.

By the 1970s a third generation of ploughs had been adapted to the greater traction available. Peat soils were drained by ditch draining ploughs which made a cut down to 15 inches to lower the water table and to provide an extra 12 inch mound in which to plant the tree. Iron pan ploughs cut down from 18 inches to three feet for the first time, rupturing the deeper pans, cultivating the soil and leaving a substantial mound of earth that suppressed weeds and in the side of which seedlings were planted. Traction came from the powerful Caterpillar D7 tractor or the very heavy 80 bhp Ford four-wheel-drive tractor, a massive machine, which on 20 inch wide flotation tyres could go over a bog, and which could deal with two hectares and more in a day.

Most of the conifers planted in Dalby Forest were already known in England but early supplies of seedlings had to come from overseas, from Japan, Canada and America until they could be produced locally. The favourite of the pre-war foresters was Scots Pine, still the dominant tree in the district. It was planted on moorland soils along with the quick growing American Lodgepole Pine, which has tended to supersede it as a more adaptable tree. Japanese and Hybrid Larch found a place on dry uplands and valley sides. Norway Spruce and Sitka Spruce took better soiled, sheltered areas but the Sitka proved capable of rapid growth in wet ground even on poor moorland and would eventually become the most generally planted tree.

In 1950, many early plantings of Sitka Spruce were still 'in check' and patches of Allerston Moor showed only a few trees which had hardly grown at all in 15 years, though with an occasional giant among the dwarfs. Later plantings showed fewer failures as experience was gained. Good results came on High Moors with Scots Pine, Corsican Pine and Lodgepole Pine. Douglas Firs found a place among the larch and spruce of slopes and dale bottoms. Dalby valley gained good stands of Sitka Spruce and Japanese Larch. In Flaxdale, the plateau soils took Scots Pine and the limestone-soils, Norway Spruce while the brown valley soils fostered Douglas Fir and Sitka Spruce.

Early nurseries to supply seedlings were established near work camps which allowed their intensive cultivation. One was at Birch Hall, Langdale End, and another at Sneverdale, Dalby. New nurseries were opened at Broxa in 1945 but Dalby's trees now also came from other parts of Britain. Sowing was done in the early spring and the seedlings transplanted into fresh beds after a year, with two inches between plants and eight inches between the rows. At 18 months to three years old, they were moved again to the prepared plantation ground, the pines four to eight inches high and other seedlings from one to four feet high. They were netted against sheep, rabbits and hares. In 1950 it was said that one man could plant 25000 seedlings a week at Broxa, and 25 million plants a year were being produced. Weeding was the main problem in the early nurseries, consuming much time and labour by men and women workers. Changes came with the mechanisation of the nurseries. Sneverdale was abandoned as a nursery in c1962 having remained weed-infested and proving too small to accommodate tractors.

The early forest workers lived chiefly at the market town and in the villages. As more land was acquired, plantings spread more widely and more villages were drawn on, but journeys to work remained lengthy and much time was spent moving around the forest. Fifty acres of Douglas Fir, Silver Fir and Norway Spruce were planted in Newton Dale in 1929. In the previous year, the new Cropton plantings drew on men discharged from the collapsing Rosedale ironstone mines. Women walked from the villages to Dalby to cut weeds with sickles. The work was remembered as long and hard.

In 1927 small agricultural holdings for forest workers were begun at Dalby. A pair of bungalows was built for £600 at Deepdale, near Bickley, two years later. Ten acres or so of grazing was attached to each house and workers who lived at the bungalows and houses at Dalby Beck, Dalby Meadow, Low Dalby Wood, Upper Dalby Wood and Nut Wood west of the beck and Low Wood east of the stream, combined the life of a smallholder with forest employment. Low Dalby House and Dalby Cottage, previously a granary, were also absorbed into forest use but the houses were scattered and did not yet form a village. Horses used in the woods were stabled on the holdings or pastured in fields near plantations being thinned.

The Commission is not known to have had its own stables and must earlier have hired farm horses.

A new source of workers was drawn on in September 1933. There was great national unemployment and a scheme was launched for the expanding forest to use batches of 200 young men selected from the unemployed of the industrial areas. A government instruction centre was built by 16 Birmingham youths who had received some vocational training and were paid 17s weekly maintenance and 3s pocket money. They came among people described as 'living quiet self contained lives, untroubled by the problems of the world outside', amidst 'a natural garden, thickly carpeted in spring with primroses and golden daffodils and ablaze in summer with an immense variety of wild flowers'. The work camp was called a 'reconditioning centre'. The army-style huts accommodated 200, who came in batches of 50 from Tyneside, Middlesbrough, Leeds, Hull, Sheffield, Durham and Birmingham. Selected from those long out of work and judged to have deteriorated in physique, they stayed for 12 weeks working on land draining, road making, cutting drains, erecting fences, trenching, removing boulders and levelling. Some had not had a job for the seven or eight years since they left school. It was intended that 'bracing air, plain living and hard work could recondition them for the labour market'.

Allerston Instructional Centre, Low Dalby, c 1934
[Copyright unknown]

WORK CAMPS FOR THE UNEMPLOYED

PRESS REPORT 1934

"The method is excellently fitted to the purpose. The huts are pleasant, airy structures with excellent sleeping accommodation. The food is plentiful and nutritious. A recreation hut, well equipped with billiard tables and popular indoor games offers opportunities for concerts and entertainment. A keen young welfare officer is attached to the staff to organise games and general recreation. There are matches with the village cricket teams. On Sunday morning, the recreation hut becomes a temporary church in which popular services are conducted by local ministers. These are always well attended and the voluntary chaplain has many opportunities of coming into personal contact with the men.

The daily work of the campers is varied and interesting. An experienced manager, assisted by a highly efficient staff, controls the centre and uses a wide discretion in the interests of the men. He is dealing with men unaccustomed to work, in some cases with men who literally have to be taught to work. Such a task demands exceptional tact and patience. The measure of success is shown by the contentment of the men. The entire scheme is of course on a voluntary basis and they are free to leave the camp if they choose, or men may be dismissed for unruly conduct. In practice such eventualities rarely occur. The men are obviously happy at the end of their three months' term. They show marked improvement in appearance and capability. Their faces glow with health and good spirits, their eyes shine with hope and determination and the grip of their hands is more assured and confident."

In fact, not all was sweetness and light. 'Some of them were a bit wild at the huts,' recalls one local. The market town of Pickering met camp workers at weekends. They walked over via Kingthorpe and the Whitby road. Tales are still told of fights, one ending when a Pickering PC bumped two heads together on one late evening. Another party returning 'full of ale' to Dalby, stripped all the pears from the front of the old Spotted Cow Inn at the fringe of Pickering. 'They hung there like bloody grapes,' said the man who lost them. Another Ministry of Labour camp was opened at Birch Hall, Langdale End in 1935. Three years later, its men started making the west side road to Langdale. At the conclusion of their stay, workers in the camps were offered places in special vocational training centres from which the chances of gaining employment were good. The huts have gone at Dalby, only a slab of concrete marking their site, but Birch Hall is now used by the Scouts as a campsite.

THE CHANGING FOREST

Acquisition of land for planting continued steadily. By 1939, the Forest District had 17 373 acres. Distant land at Scardale by Place Newton on the Wolds was bought that year and planted in 1941. The Keldy lease was purchased and extra land totalling 8 369 acres above Cropton acquired in 1948. The next year, the remainder of the Crosscliffe Estate was secured and Penny Howe, Harwood Dale was bought from Lord Downe in 1950. The acreage now exceeded 30 000 and extended far beyond the old Dalby Forest. Egton Estate land was bought in 1957 and Newton House transferred from the Ministry of Defence with 3 163 acres in 1966, taking the acreage over 40 000.

*Girls from the Women's Timber Corps did valuable
work in Dalby Forest during the Second World War.
[Photo donated to the Forestry Commission]*

Internal organisation was adjusted to this growth. The Commission divided its North York Moors and neighbouring properties into Allerston and Hambleton Forests. Allerston embraced the fairly compact lands of the Whitby-Scarborough-Kirkbymoorside area. Hambleton included detached woods in the Hambleton, Howardian and Cleveland Hills. Allerston Forest was ultimately renamed the Pickering Forest District and was really several forests plus areas of open moor and farmland. Most of its land was in the North York Moors National Park. There were outliers at Eskdale and the Wolds. Dalby, Cropton, Wykeham and Langdale became 'forests' within the Pickering Forest District, each with its Head Forester under a District Forest Officer.

Planting went forward at a different rate to land acquisition. The heaviest programmes were undertaken after the Second World War had again eaten into national timber resources. By 1950, some 13 000 acres had been planted. Other land owned was farmed or in reserve. Troutsdale and Staindale had been planted and the higher sheep walks were steadily covered with trees. Dalby long retained a reserve of land with some valley and higher ground kept for farming. Consultation with the Ministry of Agriculture sought to ensure optimum land use but as reserves narrowed, pressure to plant marginal farm land grew. Sloping land, small left-over pieces and even old quarries were also brought into use. Steep slopes proved capable of taking a mixture of conifer and broadleaf trees, though individual planting was necessary. Some land unsuitable for commercial use was planted with scrub hardwoods. By 1976 Dalby Forest had virtually exhausted all its reserves of plantable land.

Low Dalby Farm was converted to accommodate a forester and forest workers and its scattered buildings eventually became offices, hall, museum and public toilets. The Ings land along the valley was attached to the forest workers' homesteads built in the fields. John Coulson left High Dalby Farm c1940, moving to Full Sutton where his son had a poultry farm. A Mr Smith moved in briefly and is credited with ploughing up the garden to get the new potato planting subsidy. Then senior forest officers moved in, District Officers Mr Peter Garthwaite and Mr Stott, who sweated out the severe winter of 1947, and Mr Condor, another District Officer. As local housing became less scarce, it ceased to be used and by 1955 had begun to fall to ruin. The old tiled cottage and farm was then bought with seven acres of land by Sir Meredith Whitaker, the Chairman of Scarborough District Newspapers Ltd. For some years he used it as a summer house but, fearful of Coulson's 'formidable acetylene gas installation', made do with paraffin lamps. In 1966-7, he converted the two dwellings into an imposing house. A new interior was installed, as far as possible within the existing walls, though the place had earlier been added to at different times. Electricity and a less erratic water supply were installed. It remained possible to identify the one up, one down, modest original farmstead, for three internal walls had clearly once been external, while the wall between the original kitchen and Coulson's added dining room was over two feet thick. A wooden staircase had run up at a hair-raising angle from the kitchen to the bedroom above. The house stands in its own ground athwart Dalby Beck and feeder streams.

High Riggs Farm became independent of High Dalby. It lost the west end of Stoneclose Rigg to plantations in 1939 and Newclose Rigg in the early forties. Farmers felt that some of the better land should have remained agricultural. Some old shelter belts were removed but the exposed character of the site ended as they were replaced by growing woodland. It became a compact holding encompassed by trees. Once said to have had the run over 1 400 acres, it was by 1969 a farm of 240 acres, largely arable and, interestingly enough, in the same general area where in Roman British times the earliest Dalby farming may well have taken place. A quern for milling corn was found here by Miss Laley.

In that year, the farmer David Laley who was working the farm with his sons said 'I grow mainly barley but also sow turnips, rape and swedes'. The farm had 25 cross beef cattle, Friesian, Angus and Hereford and 500 ewes. These were mainly Mashams but with a few Swaledale and some Teeswater tups and 'we also keep some poultry for ourselves'. He also had 50 homing pigeons. Water was now pumped to the farm from Low Dalby and some 3 000 gallons stored. Picnickers breaking fences and running after sheep were one problem, consumption of crops by fox, badger, roe and the occasional red deer another, while in the winter the farm might be cut off by snowdrifts for three weeks. One year they had to dig themselves out four times.

In 1976 Riggs Farm remained active, while some 40 forestry workers' holdings with about ten acres each attached to a homestead were scattered about the district, some at Jingleby. Some farm holdings were due to be planted but others were being improved and moulded into more viable units for full time farmers. Most of Dalby's small area of reserve land would be planted up within a few years.

As the young plantations matured, the close planted trees rose tall, closing up to exclude wind and the light that fostered competing plant life. As lower branches died off, they were 'brashed' or cut away to reduce the risk of fire and to give cleaner poles and timber. On good locations, straight stems reached high. Trees might not mature for 40, 50 or even 70 years but after 20 years, thinning could begin to encourage the best stems and to give a marketable crop of small wood. Thinning began in 1938 but sustained thinning had to wait another ten years. Thereafter, at regular intervals every five or six years, a fresh yield of thinnings was taken. Over a plantation's life, density might fall from 1 500 to 50 trees to an acre.

Wood from thinnings was sent chiefly as pit props for the Yorkshire coal mines, or as fencing stakes, rails and posts for farms, but telegraph posts, garden poles and pulpwood for the hardboard mills on Teesside were also produced. Even as the trees grew, the old sources of demand had altered. Railway demand had slackened as sleepers and wagon bottoms were made of steel instead of timber as the rail network shrank. Many industries once using wood had turned to plastic. There was contraction in the coal industry too but the Yorkshire mines still generated a strong demand for pit props. New demand was for soft woods rather than hard for sawn timber, for larch poles and fences, spruce for pulps and woodwool for packing. Later thinning and eventual clear felling produced logs for the sawmills, planks for the builder and fully-grown wood for a vast range of uses. With the nation importing 92% of its annual wood consumption, the 3rd largest import after food and fuel, at a bill in of £1 800 000 000, the potential contribution of forests to the national economy was enormous.

Output from Pickering Forest District (in cubic metres)

	1971 -2	1972-3	1973-4
Thinning	17 720	19 200	18 550
Felling	4 570	8 970	11 110
Total	22 290	28 170	29 660

(1974 estimates for the Commission's production were:- pit wood 36%, sawn logs 29%, pole lengths 18%, posts, stakes and rails 8%, pulp wood 2%)

Thinning and felling in the early days was by the axe and cross-cut saws. Some felling was done in anticipation of windblow. One man with a bow saw could fell 40 trees of 3-4in diameter and peel them in a day. Horses were used by the Commission to pull out thinnings between the standing trees until the 1950s and Mr Ted Corney of Dalby had some of the last to be used. In 1974, the Commission sold 37% of the total crop to timber merchants who cut the wood themselves and some still used teams of horses to pull out thinnings. Speaking in 1969, Mr T Jakimow, a Polish born foreman of the Pickering sawmills said that 'if they are too heavy for the horses, they are cut in half on the spot; if light several are brought at once. Felled trees may be only 3 cubes or up to 15 cubes. The cube or cubic foot is the timber man's equivalent of a hand to a groom'. One man one horse was the usual team. The horses were heavy Clydesdales or clean-legged Clevelands. Their equipment was the traditional bridge, with blinkers, halter, a short hame rein against stumbling and a collar with iron hames attached. From its hooks, the trace chains passed via a back band to stop dropping when slack. They were kept from nipping the legs by a stretcher. From end to end of the stretcher was attached a short length of trace chain. Onto this was hung the 'snigging' chain, the hook of which passed round and under the timber and then through its own ring. As the horse moved, it tightened round the load. Bill Rawson of Ebberston was contractor for the horses.

A revolution in thinning, felling and hauling came in the late 1950s. With the advent of the petrol-engine chain saw in 1958, one man could cut down 100 thinnings a day instead of 40. Commission workers dealt with 63% of the total crop in 1974. The German Holder A20 tractor, with its 3ft 10in track, four-wheel-drive and wasp waist, originally developed for use in the vineyards, was brought into use in 1969. Half a ton was a horse load but the tractor, narrow, stable and more powerful, could pull 5 tons at a go. Tractors and winches made the horse a rarity. Four-wheel-drive tractors were now used with double drum winches to skid poles to the roadside. Where slopes were steep and access difficult, cable cranes were used for extraction, the cable hauled in and out on a double drum winch mounted on a tractor. Peeling machines and circular splitting saws also came into use.

Tractors, heavy ploughs, powered saws and other equipment meant mechanisation of forestry work. As the lumberjack image faded, skilled technicians replaced labourers. The machine operator took the place of the wood cutter. A forest worker training scheme started at Birch Hall in 1947 and more elaborate training became essential as equipment became sophisticated. Even the nurseries were mechanised and a dozen men with equipment and chemicals supplied the seedlings that once eighty or ninety workers produced. Where ten men took two hours to load a vehicle, two men could load a timber lorry in half an hour using a tractor-mounted hydraulic grapple. As forestry ceased to be a labour intensive industry, the number of workers fell, though the acreage increased. Where 45 men had been needed full time in Dalby Forest, now 25 were enough. Fewer workers could handle greater quantities of wood at faster speeds. Twenty ton loads were hauled away daily in Commission and contractors' vehicles to Pickering and other sawmills, to Wallsend for making into chipboard or to Ellesmere for pulping. Supervision became less as administration was enlarged. The old Dalby Forest had a Head Forester, four under foresters and three gangers but now there were two under foresters, a trainee and no gangers.

Fire was a nightmare for the early foresters. In the woods and on the heather moor the danger was acute when winds were dry or in summer drought when moor walkers were numerous. Forest rides and perimeter breaks, clear of plantings or other vegetation, near moorland gave some protection. Fire patrols and lookouts, water storage tanks and fire brooms formed part of the system of prevention and control. A seventy-foot-high observation tower, sited 800ft above sea level at the highest point of the forest, was continuously manned in danger periods.

German bombs caused fires at Bickley in 1940, destroying 54 acres, and at Harwood Dale where 240 acres were lost. A large moorland fire on Fylingdales Moor in 1942 was halted just short of the Langdale plantation edge. Another extensive fire at Derwent Head in 1949 was extinguished before it reached the trees. Cropton lost 35 acres as a result of lightning in 1952 and there is talk of a fire damaging 100 acres somewhere near Upper Dalby in 1958. Japanese Larch is highly resistant to fire and plantations of this tree divide the forest. Older trees are less susceptible than young plantations but rising visitor traffic increased the risks.

Many miles of new roads were made, some 220 miles in the Pickering Forest District to give access to forest 'compartments'. Even more numerous were the straight 'forest rides'. Some followed older tracks but as plantations extended the new network became largely independent of the old. The Georgian and Victorian quarries where farmers graved lime for burning to put on the acid soils were supplemented by new roadstone workings. The road up Staindale was surveyed before the war. Raymond Walton of Pickering helped as a boy. It was laid with chippings in 1938-9 but has since become the Forest Drive. Access to Low Dalby for wheeled traffic long remained via Ellerburn, for the old Haygate was a poor track until metalled after the war. For the later roads, tarmac and crushed stone were brought in. The old earth roads that John Cross used when he galloped on his pony from Dalby to the school at Thornton Dale disappeared. They were happier places in fair weather than foul and in some winters riders for Dalby could not tell when they crossed a gate or hedge, the drifts were so deep. Metalled roads made with modern bulldozers and grading machines gave ready access in all seasons. The District estate, civil and mechanical engineering depots and the vehicle depot and workshop were near Low Dalby.

The forest rides gave access to all compartments for management and were not made up. They served a limited role as firebreaks. Most were made 40 or 60 feet wide and they were now maintained by a 'brushcutter', pulled by a four-wheel-drive tractor. Mowing was regulated to conserve ground flora. The machine could cover several miles in a day. With the opening of the Forest Drive to the public, a new quality of through road was called for. The Commission ceased to lock the gate to keep people out in 1960 but the road remained untarmaced until a road toll was levied to pay for the improvement. Now, with more developed through-roads, car parks and picnic areas, parts of the forest acquired a park-like appearance. Here and there an anomaly survived from historical times. The old Overscar Lane, locally 'Ovisker' is a country road at the top and is infrequently resurfaced by the County Council, about as far as the gate to Rose cottage now renamed Staindale Lodge. The Forestry Commission maintains the low road through the pasture as far as the farm gate. Between the country road and the Commission road is a stretch that appears to be no-man's land.

With the completion of the first plantings, the history of Dalby Forest moved on from its first 'afforestation' phase. In the next stage, old plantings of different date reached maturity and full grown trees would supply a wider range of uses. Thinning continued but final harvesting had supplanted it as the main activity of the forest. About 60% of the forest was now in the formative stage but before 1980, it was expected that more timber would come from felling than thinning. Dalby yielded 21 000 cubic metres of timber in a year from its 3 334 hectares. This would rise to 30 000 cubic metres by 1986, equivalent to six large wagonloads for every working day of the year.

As clear-felling became more general, good second rotation crops were needed. Their planting was well under way at Dalby. Local experimental areas were set up in 1967 to determine the best successor crops. More demanding yet more productive species, particularly Sitka Spruce were being planted on sites which earlier carried larch and pine. The modern heavy-duty machines made light work of iron pan and old tree stumps alike. Species were more closely matched to each site. A valuable soil survey was prepared for the whole forest in 1967 and research in 1968 was designed to test the stability of trees in diverse soils by tree-pulling.

Alteration of the soil by fertilizers was increasingly important. Mineral phosphate additions were tried at Langdale in 1938 but the amount, one ounce to the tree, was too small. The first application of GMP fertilizer from the air was tried on 850 acres at Langdale in 1968, and another 865 acres at Cropton were treated in 1969. Three hundredweight of phosphate to the acre was being dropped in 1976. Weed control in young plantations since the war became a matter of selective killing by sprays between rows about a year after planting. The restocking of clear-felled areas allowed a new weed growth. Pests remained a problem. Rabbits devastated newly planted areas frequently until the myxomatosis outbreak in 1953-4 reduced their population but fringe woods became affected again since. In 1934 there was heavy pine-saw fly infestation at Dalby, the caterpillar eating off all but the current year's needles and preventing trees reaching maximum growth. It returned to defoliate areas of Langdale and Broxa Moor in 1948. Grey squirrels remained a serious menace, killing trees by stripping their bark.

THE VILLAGE OF LOW DALBY

Mr Jerry Warriner of Pickering recalled boyhood visits to his uncle at Jingleby and others of this family at High Staindale Farm. His grandfather spent two days on horseback getting sheep in from as far as Bickley for dipping. The lad spent days scruffling turnips and, on one occasion, three hours turning a churn to make butter which was stored in the ground below Staindale spring. It was mainly a sheep farm but there were cornfields on the high ground and a few cows in the valley for milk. Breakfast was at 5.30am and days were long. The huckster called once a week for eggs. Turf cuttings were like harvest time and through the year the lad 'sniggled' rabbits with copper wire, for cartridges were dear.

It was a vanishing way of life. In another decade, Mr Warriner, now 25 years old, worked for the Thornton Dale Co-operative Stores. About 1935, he would pushbike up the unmetalled and gated road from Ellerburn to Dalby. There were 13 gates to open and close. He started without much custom but made eleven calls to seek it at the farm and forestry holdings. When he finished, 3½ tons of stuff were going up the dale every week, from paraffin to provisions. The dale was changing.

Just before the War it was decided to develop a small village for forestry workers in the area where the work camps had been near Low Dalby House. There were already six scattered farm holding houses as well as Low Dalby House and Low Dalby Cottage. Newer houses were built in 'terraces' in 1949, contrasting in style with the old farm buildings and older houses, and given numbers instead of names. Other forest settlements were made at Langdale and at Darncombe. Mr Wilf Dodsworth took a new Dalby house as the first tenant. For many years he would run the shop and sub post office and the village grew around him.

The small community developed with its own way of life. The only resident not working in the forest in 1969 was Mr B Hopper, a driving instructor. Thirty-five others did draw their income from the forest. He thought that 'with everyone doing the same jobs the communal spirit was really remarkable'. In 1967 they began a social club in the farm building that was converted into a village hall. There was an annual fete, domino drives, an illuminated tree at Christmas, a children's playground and a car park that doubled as a tennis court. Children went to school at Thornton Dale. Fuel was plentiful and snowploughs kept the roads open during the winter. In 1976 there were 18 houses with 60 adults and children at Low Dalby, but the post office had closed as part of the contraction of services in rural areas.

CONSERVATION AND RECREATION – THE VISITOR WELCOMED

One of the more dramatic and at first unrealised effects of the forest planting programme was a total change in the district's wildlife. The exposed moors, the old valley side scrub woodlands, the agricultural land of the tabular hills and the valley pastures had each sustained their own natural populations. As the conifers closed their canopy, the light that gave them life vanished and their habitat with it. As young forest matured, only the forest rides and roads or the green canopy carried any vigorous wildlife. Yet it would overspill again as thinning began and new colonies of plants, animals, birds and insects could re-conquer the mature forest. Yet, with clear felling their habitat would be destroyed and the cycle would start again.

Rabbits were treated as pests and their breeding and feeding grounds attacked. Wood pigeons stayed common along the rides, and the closeness of the old Kingthorpe woods enriched the bird life. Badger and fox were common still but the creatures of the open ground moved away. Myxamatosis took the rabbit and the buzzards and other predators that fed on him. Pheasants long reared since Victorian times at Allerston found a home and coal tits hugged the canopy. Then as the forest changed, discoveries were made. A roe deer was first seen by an old Allerston warrener, Mr Parry of Lockton at Dalby's Housedale in 1936. The herd grew and, with damage to tree bark by browsing and fraying, control of the worst offenders had to be introduced. Deer had become largely extinct outside parks by the mid 19th century, but escapes of fallow deer from Aldby Park during World War II are believed to have taken them to Ampleforth Forest while further north some red deer escaped from the Duncombe Park herd. Roe deer, which are very fond of young plantations, saw a veritable population explosion.

In 1965, the Forestry Commission recognised that a changed public attitude to wildlife required a new balance to be struck between the need to prevent damage to trees and the need for wildlife conservation. In the huge maturing forests, total prevention of damage was in any case impracticable. A policy of humane selective control was introduced for animals causing damage combined with encouragement of wildlife, like the badger, that gave rise to no adverse effects or which, like the pine marten, was becoming rare. Pests remained pests and were treated as such. Grey squirrels were an increasing source of damage and hares were shot. Badgers were encouraged and nesting boxes placed for redstarts, tits and flycatchers. Deer were selectively controlled by skilled marksmen using rifles to shoot the most damaging individuals. The key to deer population is the number of does that survive the winter, yet if the balance of sexes in a herd is upset, wandering bucks looking for does can do even greater damage. The use of experienced stalkers to do some culling brought extra revenue and the shooting was let subject to strict controls. Does were culled from November to February and old bucks past their prime in May. Game shooting was also leased, usually for three-year periods, but with provisos that the head of game must be maintained and nests protected by the control of vermin. In c1964, Mr Gordon Simpson, as Forest Warden, made a detailed record of the plant, animal and insect life of the forest (In 2007 and in his mid-seventies Mr Simpson was still carrying out extensive wildlife surveys for the Forestry Commission in Northumberland and is widely regarded as one of the North of England's best all-round naturalists). Later, a conservation forester and five rangers in the District had a dual responsibility for protecting the trees from damage by wildlife and to diversify and protect wildlife itself.

Another change in public attitudes and needs came in the sphere of recreation as the young forests matured. In the early days, public access was only allowed along surviving public footpaths. Ramblers found little to interest them in young plantations but a Youth Hostel at Low Staindale and pretty valleys like Dalby continued to attract picnickers. The Hostel, in a house reputedly 350 years old, closed in 1966. Thornton Dale between the wars remained popular for staying holidaymakers, many of them country lovers, who were urged by local guidebooks to walk up the valley by Ellerburn to High Dalby and the Bridestones, or to take the paths up Hawdale and Sandale to Givendale. Keen naturalists sought badgers, otters and snakes in Dalby Valley or penetrated to the heronry in Staindale.

After the Second World War, a better living standard brought far more visitors, by new means of transport - the long distance coach and the motor car rather than the railway train and bicycle. Indeed, Thornton Dale lost its railway station. Motor cars took staying visitors and day-trippers further afield, whether 'grouse moor men' or anglers. Increased numbers came to Dalby, sparking off a rights of way dispute at High Dalby that ran on from 1955 to 1965. The old roads had stood the occasional stallion or threshing machine but were ill-adapted to the new traffic. Facilities were slight and there were complaints of litter and gates left open. Sheep were killed by cars on moor roads and it was some time before a positive attitude to tourists emerged. Neither residents nor the Forestry Commission recognised the new industry that was emerging and which could benefit a country district, where farm employment and rural industries were in decline.

The North York Moors National Park formed in 1952 brought some recognition of a need to provide facilities for public recreation in the countryside. Though its boundaries were drawn to include all of old Dalby, the village of Thornton Dale and much other forest land, it was initially largely concerned with negative planning control. The Forestry Commission took a fresh look at the role of its forests in the national life in 1963. One result was greater attention to the open air recreation that forests could offer. Visitor problems were not altogether unfamiliar. Girl Guide campers had enjoyed holidays at Dalby back in 1942-3 but they had come for a fortnight's work brashing and weeding. In 1959 a school campsite had opened at Dalby and a scout campsite at Birch Hall (This latter was still run by Scarborough and District Scouts in 2007, the main building being a carefully restored hut from the 1930s 'Instructional Centre'). The spring of 1960 saw a much more dramatic experiment. A Forest Drive for motorists was opened starting at Low Dalby and running to Bickley, whence the county road continued to Hackness. The first RAC rally used the forest two years later.

The Dalby experiment played its part in the Commission's reappraisal. Positive steps began to be taken to encourage visitors to go to beauty spots, and to provide facilities where these would yield an economic return. Arguing that it cost £3 000 a year to maintain a motor road and to provide such facilities as ornamental trees, forest trails and other amenities to make the visitors' experience more pleasurable, it was decided to levy a toll of 4s a car on the Forest Drive in 1969. There was an outburst of criticism from local people, who felt their established rights of way were being intruded upon, and others who said that state forests belonged to the people and should be free. The critics were largely disarmed by the improvement that followed.

A Sneverdale Forest Trail was opened in August 1964, arranged to display how a forest develops. Along the walk was an area of inverted turf planted with young trees, a nursery of Christmas trees and examples of pruning, brashing and making a thinning. The Trail was instantly popular and others were made at Silpho and Wykeham in 1965. During five hours at Easter 1969, one thousand cars passed along the improved Forest Drive at Dalby. Traffic was normally more gentle yet the whole Forest District welcomed some 300 000 visitors during 1973. In the year ending March 31st 1975 over 35 000 cars traversed the Dalby Forest Drive and 8 500 made use of a new Newton Dale Drive which offered the only car access to that beautiful and lonely valley.

The Forest proved capable of absorbing large numbers of people without appearing to do so. The grass-banked streams of Dalby proved a delight to children who swung overstream on ropes hung from trees or who paddled the beck. Adults appreciated the sheer experience of the drive among mature forest with its many delightful viewpoints. The District soon had four trails, a fifteen mile walk taking seven hours from Reasty to Allerston, and several short way-marked walks. Besides providing essential amenities such as car parks, picnic sites with tables made at the Dalby workshops, and a small museum at Low Dalby illustrating forest work and wildlife, the Commission actively encouraged more specialist interests. Four miles of the Dalby beck were available to day ticket fishermen, the wild stock of trout being supplemented annually with 10-inch fish from the Ellerburn hatchery. The angler sees the grey heron, and the kingfisher gathering its daily bag of trout in a flash of dazzling blue. There were other facilities for shooting, pony trekking, riding, nature study, orienteering, camping, car rallies and school study visits. A village café opened at Low Dalby and the village hall was adapted for use by parties. Plans were in prospect for caravan sites and forest cabins. In 1976, the Staindale Lake was opened as a combined picnic and conservation area, to add a new major attraction outside the Dalby valley.

Public response to the opening of the forest was remarkable. Misty days at the coastal resorts brought streams of cars along the drive. Some 50 000 forest trail guides were sold each year and 5 000 maps for visitors to the forest district. Wildlife pamphlets sold. Over 200 visiting parties from schools, colleges and universities came during 1975. Yet many other visitors stayed by their cars on the drives, leaving the bulk of the forest for those seeking for nature and solitude. The Conservation Forester summed it up by saying that 'today, all visitors to Dalby are welcome to find peace and quiet or to enjoy the fine scenery; all that is asked is that the country code is followed – nothing to be left save footprints, and nothing to be removed save photographs and memories'.

Dalby Forest, covering about 10 200 acres, produces timber for the nation. Back in 1876 the local Malton Gazette newspaper reported that a 'steam drag' had been tried out at Thornton Dale and had 'amazed the gazing rustics spread around'. In 1976, at a Dalby Forest Open Day 5 000 visitors came to see the results of a later technical revolution in the Forest at Dalby. Not only does Dalby produce timber but in doing so it has created a new environment of great natural beauty, in a landscape that has changed so many times before.

6

DALBY - THE PRESENT DAY

The preceding chapters written by John Rushton record the great changes that have taken place in and around Dalby Forest over several thousand years. These changes are the result of three major influences: time, natural events and lastly, and perhaps most importantly, human intervention. Things have not changed since John wrote his original book in 1976 except that society is more conscious than ever that human intervention is probably increasing the frequency and severity of natural events. Only time will tell. Management of Dalby Forest has to deliver targets set by central government in ways that benefit and reflect the needs of local and regional communities. These can be communities of place such as Thornton le Dale or communities of interest such as cyclists and ramblers or local authorities such as Ryedale District Council and the North York Moors National Park Authority.

Pine and birch on Pexton Moor in 2005
[Brian Walker, Forestry Commission]

MANAGING TREES

The present 'Dalby Forest' stretches from Ellerburn in the south to Crosscliff in the north and from Darncombe in the east to Lockton in the west covering an area of approximately 3 597 hectares or 8 888 acres. The harvesting and replanting of trees is carried out according to details laid out in the Dalby Forest Design Plan. The plan is discussed and agreed with consultees from all walks of life including the North York Moors National Park Authority, Natural England, English Heritage, neighbours, residents, local and user groups. The plans reflect changes in how the forest is used, a greater awareness of environmental issues and possible changes in future timber markets. There has been a reduction in the area of forest devoted to growing conifers while the amount of broadleaved woodland and open space has increased.

The forest crop by species and area in 2007 (See also Appendix 14)

Coniferous trees	Area (ha)	Broadleaved trees	Area (ha)
Corsican pine	107	Alder	5
Douglas fir	236	Ash	9
European larch	9	Beech	116
Grand fir	7	Birch	20
Hybrid larch	236	Mixed broadleaves	153
Japanese larch	357	Oak	26
Lodgepole pine	23	Sycamore	26
Mixed conifer	32		
Norway spruce	85	**Open space**	616
Scots pine	470	This is the area of	
Sitka spruce	1058	designated open space	
Western hemlock	10	and includes	
		agricultural land,	
		recreation and	
		conservation areas. It	
		does not include the	
		open space along	
		forest roads and rides	
		that account for about	
		5% of the forest area	

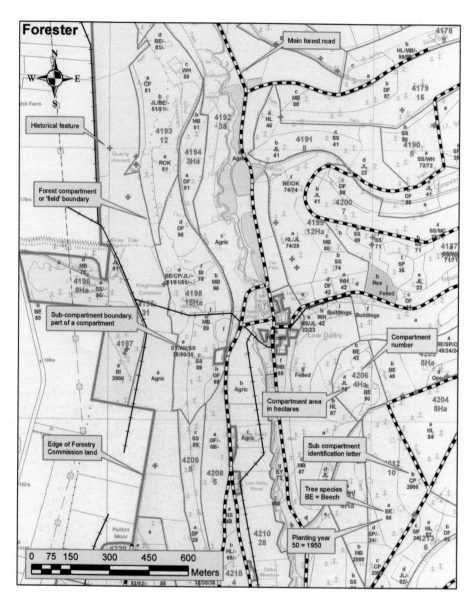

Part of the Forestry Commission stock map for Dalby Forest, recording land use, area, tree species and age

Dalby Forest is divided into management units known as 'compartments'. Initial planting practice saw the creation of compartments with the mainly artificial straight-edged boundaries that people variously call 'rides' or 'fire-breaks'. Some of the rides were almost a mile long. The imposition of such a regimented forest on the landscape proved very unpopular with some people. During the past thirty years Dalby Forest has been undergoing a process of change that has seen compartment edges broken up and a re-designing of them to reflect landscape values rather than the drawn line. Tree felling areas can cut into more than one compartment when this restructuring of the forest is taking place. Areas of felling and replanting are known as 'coups'. The soils in Dalby Forest permit the growing of a wide range of tree species but at the time of the initial planting only those that produced the highest, quickest yield of timber were planted, reflecting the urgent need for a supply of timber. Government policy at the beginning of the 21st century still requires the Forestry Commission to produce a supply of timber. This has to be a sustainable supply. Social and environmental needs also have to be recognised. All the parts of Dalby Forest that are recorded as having continuous woodland cover from 1600 to the present day are being returned to a cover of native trees and shrubs. Most of this land is along the valley side opposite Low Dalby village and along Crosscliff Brow on the northern edge of the forest. Coniferous forest will continue to play the major role in the production of the timber supply. However, this is more focussed and very invasive conifers such as western hemlock are gradually being removed.

Traditional conifer forest management in the twentieth century was centred around a clear-cut or clear felling regime. This involved the planting of a compartment of trees usually of one or two species. The growing trees would be cared for until at around twenty-five years old some of the crop would be removed in a process known as thinning. The crop would then be thinned at intervals of approximately five years until the trees reached fifty to sixty years old. The final crop would then be cleared completely from the site which would then be prepared and replanted. In the last thirty years there has been increasing interest in forest management of silvicultural systems that are less disruptive to the environment. Such techniques go under a variety of names such as Continuous Cover Forestry (CCF), Alternatives to Clear Fell (ACF) and Less Intrusive Silvicultural Systems (LISS). In these systems individual or small groups of trees are felled from within the crop and naturally occurring seedlings are recruited to fill the gaps. In Dalby Forest at the time of writing 839 hectares or around 30% of the total wooded area is designated for management in this way. Both clear felling and continuous cover systems have benefits and drawbacks for timber production and wildlife.

MANAGING PEOPLE

When the Forestry Commission was first formed in 1919 there was no intention to create major public access areas or provide the wide range of social benefits available in forests today. However Argyll Forest Park, in Scotland, where public access was freely available, was created in 1935, some sixteen years before the opening of Britain's first National Park, the Peak District in 1951. Today access to forests for all is a major part of the Forestry Commission's remit from Government. In England two forests were at the forefront of access to the countryside, Grizedale Forest in the Lake District and Dalby Forest on the edge of the North York moors. The 1960s and early 1970s saw the creation of a forest drive, a visitor centre, picnic places and waymarked walking trails in Dalby Forest. These proved highly successful.

Recent years have seen many changes in the way access to, and use of, Dalby Forest is managed and promoted. Concerns about the effect of the motor vehicle on the environment mean that a Forest Drive is no longer promoted. People are

A new environmentally-friendly visitor centre was opened
in Dalby in 2007 [Brian Walker, Forestry Commission]

encouraged to park up and leave their cars. There has been a huge increase in the number of people wanting to experience cycling away from busy roads. In recognition of this demand a series of cycle routes has been constructed using environmentally sustainable techniques. Routes vary in difficulty from 'family friendly' to 'extreme'. Children's play areas are provided at Sneverdale and

Adderstone in the hope that children who have enjoyable forest experiences will grow into adults who have a feeling of 'ownership' of the forest and continue to care for it. The quest for 'adrenaline burst' enjoyment has resulted in the development of the 'Go-Ape' high wire course where participants have to find their way through the tree tops suspended from trees.

When first opened, Dalby Forest Information Centre was located in the old farm buildings at Low Dalby. It remained there in various guises until 2007 when a new centre incorporating visitor displays, education room, restaurant and toilets, was opened in the valley at the foot of Sneverdale. The new building, of contemporary design, was constructed using timber from sustainably managed forests, the majority being from local woodlands including those at Dalby. Recycled products such as plastic bottles, wellington boots and mobile phone covers are used throughout the building in the form of doors, worktops and panels. The building has a modern heat management system, moving excess heat to cooler spaces and controlling output from the wood-fuelled boiler. The building also generates some of its own electricity through the use of photo-voltaic cells (solar panels) and a small wind turbine. The purpose of the building is to provide visitors with information about the forest while at the same time demonstrating how everyone can be more environmentally friendly. The building is designed for easy removal at the end of its life and has no concrete foundations.

The old visitor centre and the surrounding buildings at Low Dalby have become a small business courtyard with cycle hire, café, glass and arts-and-crafts workshops.

As well as providing social benefits through public access to forests the Forestry Commission also has a remit to manage the forests in its care efficiently and provide economic benefits where possible to the wider community. The influx of visitors to Dalby Forest generates trade for local businesses and accommodation providers in the forest, in Thornton le Dale and Pickering, and in the surrounding villages. During the Foot and Mouth Disease outbreak of 2001 Dalby Forest was closed for a short period and then re-opened providing a much needed tourist attraction in the area when almost all other land was closed to access to protect livestock.

In the autumn of 2002 the Forestry Commission organised a meeting of interested parties with the idea of setting up a 'Dalby Forest user group'. The Friends of Dalby Forest was formed. It has its own officers and committee and the funds it raises through the sale of season tickets to the forest are used to provide a range of facilities, events and activities independently of the Forestry Commission. It provides another way of giving forest users a voice in how the forest is managed.

Activity/Event	No. of people
General public day visits	400000*
Motor rallies	544
Cycle events	966
Sponsored walks	591
Horse riding groups	162
Orienteering events	529
Educational visits – ranger led	2877
Educational visits – self led	2743
Other group events – e.g. Community groups	1371
Search & Rescue Team Events	191
Group Camping	1339

Approximation based on calibrated vehicle numbers and occupancy

MANAGING CULTURAL AND NATURAL HERITAGE

The preceding chapters describe how the Dalby valley has evolved over the last several thousand years. This evolution was brought about by human and natural activities. Evidence of these activities can be found throughout the forest. This wide-ranging cultural and natural heritage resource is taken into account during the planning and operation of all forestry and recreational activities. Records of all features are maintained, and information is exchanged with other bodies such as the North York Moors National Park Authority, English Heritage and the North and East Yorkshire Environmental Data Centre.

Most of the prehistoric cultural sites such as burial mounds and linear earthworks are Scheduled Monuments and have statutory protection as do a number of later features particularly those associated with the rabbit warrening industry. Early field walls, parish and enclosure boundaries such as Wetmoor and Red Dikes, enclosure and ownership marker stones are all monitored and management work to protect them takes place on a regular basis. The Forestry Commission's own history, forest housing, early forest planning and management are also subject to conservation.

'Modern' archaeology: the Ordnance Survey triangulation pillar at Jingleby [Brian Walker, Forestry Commission]

Protected cultural history in Dalby Forest

Feature	No. recorded	No. Scheduled
Prehistoric round barrows	74	44
Prehistoric square barrows	1	1
Prehistoric long barrows	1	1
Prehistoric cairns	13	4
Prehistoric cemetery	1	1
Prehistoric pit alignment	2	2
Prehistoric linear earthwork	22	15
Other boundaries	6	1
Rabbit warrening features	110	11
Post mediaeval boundary markers	18	
Mid-20th century Forestry Commission Houses	19	
Pre-20th century buildings and enclosures	18	
Quarries pits and lime workings	87	
Total recorded features	372	

The creation of a new forest at Dalby in the 20th century brought about huge changes to the natural environment. Woodland creates a very different environment than that arising from intensive rabbit warrening. The last 30 years has seen the recognition that Dalby Forest is not a 'conifer plantation' but a complex mosaic of habitats. The maintenance of the mosaic is a cornerstone of forest management.

Some of the habitats found in Dalby in 2007 based on United Kingdom Biodiversity Action Plan definitions.

Habitat	Priority	Broad
Inland rock outcrop and scree	✓	
Lowland mixed deciduous woodland	✓	
Ponds	✓	
Upland calcareous grassland	✓	
Upland heathland	✓	
Upland mixed ashwoods	✓	
Upland oakwood	✓	
Wet woodland	✓	
Acid grassland		✓
Boundary & linear features		✓
Bracken		✓
Built up areas and gardens		✓
Calcareous grassland		✓
Coniferous woodland		✓
Dwarf shrub heath		✓
Fen, marsh, swamp		✓
Improved grassland		✓
Neutral grassland		✓
Rivers, streams		✓
Standing open water		✓

Interest in the natural history of Dalby Forest and the its management has increased significantly in the last thirty or so years. The importance of the broad habitats and species associated with them is recognised and taken into account before any forest operations take place through a process of environmental assessment. Priority habitats and species receive special attention and sites are identified in the Dalby Forest Design Plan. There are four Sites of Special Scientific Interest (SSSI) including Ellerburn Bank, which is one of the few remaining extensive fragments of species-rich limestone pasture in the North York Moors National Park. Ellerburn Bank is managed as a nature reserve by the Yorkshire Wildlife Trust.

Birds are generally easy to identify and they respond quickly to changes in environmental circumstance. Some adapt well and others not at all. The Forest Bird Study Group and members of the East Yorkshire Ringing Group have been studying birds across the forest. Birds that are declining nationally such as bullfinch and turtle dove are recorded as being still common in the forest. Similarly the willow tit, a bird which was scarce in the area until the 1950s and in 2007 the fastest declining species in Britain, is still a fairly common resident of the Dalby Valley. Some bird species do very well in conifer forests. Crossbills are widespread and resident in most years feeding on the seeds in the pine and larch cones. Nightjars nest on sites where the trees have been clear-felled and continue to use these sites until the next tree crop blankets the ground.

Mammal populations are difficult to assess. Roe deer are common throughout the forest but red and fallow are not resident. Badgers and foxes are very common though rarely seen by most visitors. Grey squirrels are common in the forest, as they are almost everywhere. Woodmice, field and bank voles, pigmy and common shrews are all widespread, water shrews can be found around Low Dalby and water voles, once common, seem to be an infrequent visitor. Weasels and stoats are seen from time to time and, rarely, unsubstantiated reports of pine marten are received. This animal is so seldom seen, even in the parts of the British Isles where it is common, that it is difficult to prove whether or not it truly still exists on the North York Moors. Forestry Commission rangers monitor the bat population by maintaining three bat box sites. In 2007 eight species of bat were known to be using the forest. Further down the valley Natterer's bats have a breeding roost in the little church at Ellerburn. The resulting dispute between the need to protect an endangered species and the needs of a historic church and its users has even been raised in Parliament.

Marsh Tit, a species nationally in decline but, like willow tit, common at Dalby [Chrys Mellor]

Britain has few species of reptiles and amphibians and Dalby Forest even fewer. There are good populations of adders and common lizards in suitable locations across the forest and slow-worms are plentiful. Frogs, toads and smooth newts abound especially in the old 'fire ponds' around the forest and in the big pond, known locally as Pexton or Ellers Pond built in the 1980s in the wood north of High Paper Mill Farm. Great crested newts have also been found.

There have been some interesting discoveries and changes in the invertebrate population of the area. An internationally rare whorl snail, Vertigo geyeri, is an ice age survivor in Sand Dale and the soldier fly, Odontomyia hydroleon was discovered at Seive dale. This is one of only two sites for this insect in the United Kingdom and the only English site. There have been some changes in the butterfly and dragonfly populations. Some members of both these families of insects are strong fliers and after a series of mild winters can quickly expand their range. Speckled Wood and Brimstone butterflies were unheard of in Dalby Forest in the 1970s yet 40 years on they are becoming commonplace. Of the large dragonflies only the northern and southern hawkers were common in the area. Now the ponds in the Dalby and Ellerburn area support not only these but emperor and brown hawkers as well as species of darter and skimmer dragonfly. Glow-worms can still be seen at a small number of sites in July and August.

Amongst the plants orchids always attract the most interest and the forest continues to have populations of bee and fly orchids, pyramidal orchid, greater butterfly orchid, marsh helleborine and the narrow-leaved marsh orchid. Yellow birds-nest, a plant without chlorophyll and reliant on a fungal partner that itself is reliant on Scots pine trees, occurs at a single locality.

Even the fungi of the forest have proved diverse and interesting with perhaps the rarest of all being the violet crown cup, Sarcosphaera coronaria. This is an internationally endangered species found in North America, North Africa and Southern Europe. In Dalby Forest it seems to be associated with conifers growing on lime-rich soils.

Changes in policies and management practices in recent years have ensured that Dalby Forest has remained a place of great biodiversity, that is, having a richness of wildlife. The range and distribution of species may have changed but that has been happening for millions of years.

PREPARING FOR THE FUTURE

The processes that have changed the face of Dalby over the last ten thousand years will continue in the future. Dalby will always be changing and attempts to 'preserve' the valley in any particular form will fail. Ultimately natural processes will prevail.

The violet crown cup fungus, Sarcosphaera coronaria
[Brian Walker, Forestry Commission]

CLIMATE CHANGE

The planet is warming up and has been doing so for decades, possibly centuries. It cannot be predicted how climate change will affect Dalby but a range of measures are being undertaken to ensure that the forest is as prepared as it can be for any change. The biological richness and biodiversity of the forest are being maintained and habitat networks, through which species can spread and move, are being put in place. A range of tree species is being maintained. Forest and Water Guidelines were introduced in the 1980s and increasingly management is targeted at slowing down the movement of water and keeping it on the forest. This is particularly important during torrential rain events.

THE NEED FOR WOOD

Wood has become the ultimate renewable resource, harvesting the sun's energy and locking away carbon. Its varied properties enable its use for building, papermaking, the manufacture of synthetic fabrics, and fuel. The demand for wood will grow in the future as people across the planet seek more sustainable ways of living. Future planning for Dalby includes the continued production of a sustainable supply of timber for developing markets.

THE DEMAND FOR FUEL

Using trees to produce vehicle fuel on a large scale is still some way off but there is no doubt that Dalby Forest can produce a sustainable supply of wood fuel as logs, wood chips and wood fuel pellets. Wood chips produced from trees grown in the forest already heat the visitor centre, and low-grade timber is supplied to Teesside for power station fuel. In the future it is possible that local communities such as Low Dalby, Ellerburn or Thornton Dale will receive their energy needs from wood grown in Dalby Forest.

HOW WILL PEOPLE VISIT THE FOREST?

With ever-rising fuel costs, new ways to get to the forest will need to be found. A range of cycle routes to and from the forest has been developed and public transport initiatives such as the Moorsbus will become more important. Dalby Forest Drive is no longer advertised as an attraction and people are encouraged to leave their vehicles for the day. In recent years Dalby Forest has become an important social resource contributing to the health and well-being of people from all over the region and hopefully this will continue long into the future.

Herb-rich limestone grassland near Haygate
[Brian Walker, Forestry Commission]

APPENDIX 1

The Assize of the forest 1184

This is the assize of the lord King, Henry, son of Maud, concerning the forest, and concerning his deer in England; it was made at Woodstock with the advice and assent of the archbishops, bishops, barons, earls and magnates of England.

1. First he forbids that anyone shall transgress against him in regard to his hunting-rights or his forests in any respect; and he wills that no trust shall be put in the fact that hitherto he has had mercy for the sake of their chattels upon those who have offended against him in regard to his hunting-rights and his forests. For if anyone shall offend against him hereafter and be convicted thereof he will that full justice be exacted from the offender as was done in the time of King Henry, his grandfather.

2. Item, he forbids that anyone shall have bows or arrows or hounds or harriers in his forests unless he shall have as his guarantor the King or some other person who can legally act as his guarantor.

3. Item, he forbids anyone to give or sell anything to the wasting or destruction of his own woods which lie within the forest of King Henry: he graciously allows them to take from their woods what they need, but this is to be done without wasting and at the oversight of the King's forester.

4. Item, he has commended that all who have woods within the bounds of the royal forest shall install suitable foresters in their woods; for these let those to whom the woods belong act as sureties, or let them find such suitable sureties as can give redress if the foresters shall transgress in anything which pertains to the lord King. And those who have woods without the bounds of the forest visitation, but in which the venison of the Lord King is covered by the King's peace, shall have no forester, unless they have sworn to the assize of the Lord King and to keep the peace of his hunt and to provide someone as keeper of the wood.

5. Item, the lord King has commended that his foresters shall have a care to the forest of the knights and others who have woods within the bounds of the royal forest, in order that the woods be not destroyed; for, if in spite of this, the woods shall be destroyed, let those whose woods have been destroyed know full well that reparation will be exacted from their persons or their lands, and not from another.

6. Item, the Lord King has commanded that all his foresters shall swear to maintain his assize of the forest, as he made it, according to their ability, and

that they will not molest knights or other worthy men on account of anything which the Lord King has granted them in respect of their woods.

7. Item, the King has commanded that in any county in which he has venison, twelve knights shall be appointed to guard his venison and his vert together with the forest; and that four knights shall be appointed to pasture cattle in his woods and to receive and protect his right of pannage. Also the King forbids anyone to graze cattle in his own woods, if they lie within the bounds of the forest, before the King's woods have been pastured; and the pasturing of cattle in the woods of the lord King begins fifteen days before Michaelmas and lasts until fifteen days after Michaelmas.

8. And the King has commended that if his forester shall have demense woods of the lord King in his custody, and those woods shall be destroyed, and he cannot show any just cause why the woods were destroyed, the person of the forester himself and not something else shall be seized.

9. Item, the King forbids that any clerk shall transgress either in regard to his venison or to his forests; he has given strict orders to his foresters that if they find any such trespassing there, they shall not hesitate to lay hands upon them and to arrest them and to secure their persons, and the King himself will give them his full warrant.

10. Item, the King has commanded that his assarts, both new and old, shall be inspected, and likewise both purprestures and the wastes of the forest, and that each shall be set down in writing by itself.

11. Item, the King has commanded that the archbishops, bishops, earls, barons, knights, freeholders and all men shall heed the summons of his master-forester to come and hear the pleas of the lord King concerning his forests and to transact his other business in the county court, if they would avoid falling into the mercy of the lord King.

12. At Woodstock, the King commanded that safe pledges shall be taken from any who shall be guilty of one transgression in respect of the forest, and likewise if he shall trespass a second time; but if he shall transgress a third time, for this third offence no other pledges shall be taken from him nor anything else, except the very person of the transgressor.

13. Item, the King has commanded that every male attaining the age of twelve years and dwelling within the jurisdiction of the hunt, shall swear to keep the King's peace, and likewise the clerks who hold lands in lay fee there.

14. Item, the King has commanded that the mutilation of dogs shall be carried out wherever his wild animals have their lairs and were wont to do so.

15. Item, the King has commanded that no tanner or bleacher of hides shall dwell in his forests outside of a borough.

16. Item, the King has commanded that none shall hereafter in any wise hunt wild animals by night with a view to their capture, either within the forest or without, wheresoever the animals frequent or have their lairs, or were wont to do so, under pain of imprisonment for one year and the payment of a fine or ransom at his pleasure. And no one, under the same penalty, shall place any obstruction whether alive or dead in the path of his beasts in his forests and woods, or in other places disafforested by himself and his predecessors.

APPENDIX 2

The Master of the Game c1410, by Edward, 2nd Duke of York

The Master of the Game should be in accordance with the Master Forester or Parker where it should be that the King should hunt such a day, and if the tract be wide, the aforesaid forester or parker should warn the sheriff of the Shire where the hunting shall be, for to order sufficient stable, and carts, also to bring the deer that should be slain to the place where the curees at huntings have usually been hold. And thence he should warn the hunters and fewterers whither they should come, and the forester should have men ready there to meet them that they go no farther, nor straggle about for fear of frightening the game, before the King comes. And if the hunting shall be a park, all men should remain at the park gate, save the stable that ought to be set ere the King comes, and they should be set by the foresters or parkers. And early in the morning the Master of the Game should be at the wood to see that all be ready and he or his lieutenant or such hunters that he wishes, ought to set the greyhounds, and whoso be teasers to the King or to the Queen, or to their attendants. As often as any hart comes out, he should when he passes blow a note and recheat, and let slip to tease it forth, and if it be a stag, he should let him pass as I said and rally to warn the fewterers what is coming out. And to lesser deer, should no wight let run and if he has seen the stag, not unless he were commanded. And then the master forester or parker ought to show him the King's standing, if the King would stand with his bow, and where all the remnant of the bows would stand. And the yeoman for the King's bows ought to be there to keep and make the King's standing, and remain there without noise, till the King comes. And the grooms that keep the King's dogs and broken greyhounds should be there with him, for they belong to the yeomen's office, and also the Master of the Game should be informed by the forester or parker what game the King should find within the set, and when all this is done, then should the Master of the Game worthe upon horse and meet the King and bring him to his standing, and tell him what game is within the set, and how the greyhounds be set, and also the stable, and also tell him where it is best for him to stand with his bow or with his greyhounds, for it is to be known that the attendants of his chamber and of the Queen's should be best placed, and the two fewterers ought to make fair lodges of green boughs at the tryste to keep the King and Queen and ladies and gentlewomen and also the greyhounds from the sun and bad weather. And when the King is at his standing or at his tryste, whichever he prefers, and that the Master of the Game or his lieutenant have set the bows and assigned who shall lead the Queen to her tryste, then he should blow the three long notes for the uncoupling. And the hart hounds and the harriers that before have been led by some forester or parker thither where they should uncouple, and all the hounds that belong to both the mutes (packs) waiting for the Master of the Game's blowing.

APPENDIX 3

The old dialect language of the countryside around Dalby

Animals		Birds		Insects, reptiles and others	
Angels holes	Of moles and field mice	Billybiter	Blackcap	Aisk	Newt
Backbeeraway	Bat	Bullspink	chaffinch	Blacksnake	Slow worm
Blindmouse	Shrew	Butterbump	Bittern	Cleg	Horsefly
Brock	Badger	Collier	swift	Clocks	Beetles
Catswerril	Squirrel (also used of pine marten)	Crake	Crow or rook	Hagworm	Adder
Clubster	Stoat	Cooscot (Cushet)	Wood pigeon	Jewdicow	Ladybird
Foulmart	Polecat	Dowp	Carrion crow	Lobstrous louse	Wood louse
Pait or brock	Badger	Goldspink	Yellow hammer	Lop	Flea
Pricky urichin (also 'pricky back otchen')	Hedgehog	Green linnet	Greenfinch	Midge	Gnat
Ratten	Rat	Herrinsew	Heron		
Rezzle	Weasel	Hufil	(Green) woodpecker	Sheepcade	Sheep louse
Sweetmart	Pine marten	Hulet	Owl	Sleaworm	Slow worm
		Lairock	Skylark	Twitchbell	Earwig
		Nant pie	Magpie		
		Porrd tailer	Goldfinch		
		Redtail	Redstart		
		Tom tit	Wren		
		Tufit	Peewit (Lapwing)		
		Uzzle	Blackbird		
		White nebbed crow	Rook		

Trees, Fruits and Plants

Aum	Elm	Cornbind	Climbing buckweed (Bindweed)	Pissibeds	Dandelion
Bairnworts	Daisies	Cows& calves	Cuckoo pint	Planetree	Sycamore
Bent	Rushes	Cuprose	Poppy	Quicks	Couch grass
Bluecap	Scabious			Rowantree	Mountain Ash
		Deadnettle	Wild hemp		
Bottery	Elder	Eller	Alder	Runch	Charlock
Breckon	Fern/Bracken	Esh	Ash	Scrogs	Stunted shrubs
Bulls foreheads	Hassock grass	Fitches	Vetches	Seaves	Soft rush
		Folafoot	Coltsfoot	Seggrum	Ragwort
Burthistle	Spear thistle				
Bummelkites	Blackberries	Foxfingers	Foxglove	Swidden	Burnt heath
Burk	Birch	Hollin	Holly	Wilf	Willow
Busck	Bush	Horsenobs (also Hardheads)	Knapweed	Worleberry	Bleaberry
Butterwork	Bog violet			Swine thistle	Sow thistle
		Hyvin	Ivy		
Carberries	Gooseberries	Laverocks	Wood sorrel	Whins	Furze (Gorse)
Cheescake grass	Birdsfoot trefoil	Ling	Heath (Heather)	Yack	Oak
Ciceley	Cow parsley	Moorpalms	Cotton grass		
Clock seaves	Black bogrush	Pigleaves	Meadow thistle		

On the road

Badger	A huckster or peddler	Gait	Road
Barguest	A hobgoblin	Galloway	Pony
Boggle	A lesser goblin	Loadsaddle	Packsaddle
Burdenband	Hemp hay band	Pannel	Soft packsaddle
Cadger	Carrier	Pooac	Corn bag
Coop	Oxcart	Stags	Young horses
Draught	Team of oxen or later horses	Wain	A large oxcart
Gad	7ft rod with 3ft thong to drive oxen		

On the farm

Term	Definition	Term	Definition
Aither	A ploughing	Haver	Oats
Average	Pasture of stubble after a harvest	Heaf	A sheepwalk
Backstone	Baking stone	Hog, hoggard	Lamb coming up to 1 year old
Beace	Cattle stall		
		Hogs	Pigs older than 1 year
Beeld	Shelter for stock	Hog pigs	Castrates
Bisslings	First milk of a newly calven cow	To 'mold'	To spread molehills
Blendings	Peas and beans grown together	Lamb	Young sheep
Botchet	Mead	Lib	To castrate male lambs (and calves) (Horses & pigs were gelded
Brimming	A sow ready to take the boar	Meslin	Wheat & rye mix
Carlings	Fried pease	Nut gib	Nuttinghook
Cheslip skin	Calf's bag (stomach), used in making cheese rennet	Overwelt	Sheep laid on its back in a hollow
Chimpings	Rough ground oatmeal that wore teeeth	'Old' or 'blue' milk	Skim milk
Chizzil	Bran		
		Ram	Male sheep
Clipping	Sheep shearing	Riggil	Possibly poor quality lambs
Closeteap	Male sheep with both testicles in a barrel	To 'sam'	To curdle milk for cheese
Dess	A cut of hay	Seg	Castrate bull
Dockings	Trimmings of sheep buttocks	Shearing	A sheep after shearing e.g. 1st year shearing 2nd year shearing etc
Drape	A barren cow	Scythe	Long handled, long bladed tool for mowing grass and corn
Ewe	Femal sheep	Sickle	Short handled curved blade for cutting grass
Flaycrake	A scarecrow	Skeel	Milkpail
Fog	Aftergrass	Stirks	Yearling cattle
Gilts	Young female pigs	Swine	Pigs older than 2 years
Gimmer	Female young sheep	Tup	Male sheep
Gimmer hog	Female ewe of 1st year	Wethers	Castrated male sheep
Guilefat	Vat to make ale	Whie	Young cow or heifer
Hangsteap	A male sheep		

In the landscape

Beck	Stream	Croft	Small enclosure
Crooks	Often short strips in bend of stream	Dike	Long ditch
Fallows	Ground resting without crop or sewn grass	Field	A common field containing blocks called flats, themselves containing ploughed strips. After Enclosure applied to any fenced ground.
Foldgarth	Farmyard	Foss	Waterfall
Gill	Small valley	Griff	Narrow valley
Grip	Ditch	Hagg	Coppice
Helm	Open cattle shed sometimes covered with faggots or corn	Holm	Land encompassed by water
Howe	Small hillock often a burial mound	Howl	Hollow
Garth	A small enclosure near a house	Ing	Meadow ground, often early enclosed for mowing
Keld	A Spring	Knoll	Hill top
Leylands	Tillage land left under grass	Muckmidden	Dunghill
Oskins or Oxgangs	Shares of a common field	Ploughlands	Tillage land
Rigg	Ridge	Scar	Steep exposed rock
Sike	Small boggy stream	Slack	Shallow valley
Summer-eat	Pastures	Swang	Long, wet grassy place
Thwaite	A clearing	Wath	A ford

APPENDIX 4

The Old Place-Names of Dalby

Within Dalby every feature had its old name. They could change over time but some date back to Anglian and Scandinavian times.

Dale names

Dixon's Slack	no one of the name Dixon is known, but it could come from Dickon, a pet name in the Middle Ages for Richard. A Richard of Dalby is known.
Langdale Howl	accurately describes a long hollow.
Swairdale	possibly from OE sweard meaning grass.
Staindale	perhaps from the Adderstone, once clearly visible above it.
Seivedale	from ON sef, meaning rushes. Sometimes rendered Syldale, perhaps OE syke or miry place, and sometimes Sibdale, so possibly OE personal name Sibba.
Sneverdale	sometimes rendered Shetherdale. In dialect snevver meant slender.
Keldale or Housedale	from ON keld meaning spring and the later House at Low Dalby.
Flaxdale	various suggestions have been made. In dialect flecked meant mottled, a description that might have fitted the appearance of the dale. A Scandinavian personal name Flak means fool. OE flax would refer to the plant, and linen making was an industry further down the valley.

Further south are Heckdale (sometimes Eggdale), Sandale and Hawdale. A heck was a rack, including that used for flax in dialect.

Rigg names

Adderstone Rigg	is named after the Adderstone in nearby Allerston township. This once-prominent, large natural stone, some 15ft high and 20ft across its head is on the south

brow of Staindale. In the early 19th century a fable attached to it. It is said to have the imprint of an adder or snakestone on it. Allerston itself is said to derive from Aelfhere's stone and an Arnaldeston is spoken of in mediaeval times.

Leven Hough Rigg or Lewin's Hough	possibly from ON Leofwine's hilltop or English hollow. Probably renamed New Close Rigg. New closes appear there at two places early in the 19th century, probably later than that on Stone Close Rigg.
Clenfield Rigg	sometimes Cleufield. The element 'field' suggests early cultivation and the name was in use in the 14th century. Includes Stonesclose Rigg.
Hareborough	Brough or borough suggests a pre-Anglian earthwork or inclosure.
Haverbrough Rigg	Havver suggests oats, but OE hare and ON goat have been suggested. Har also had a dialect meaning as fog or drizzle.
Sutherbruff	or Southerborough Rigg probably South Hareborough. The large rigg is comparable in size with Hareborough Rigg, two smaller riggs lying between.
Sneverdale Rigg	ON snafa, meaning a beak or spit of land, has been suggested.

Further south are Flainsey Rigg, Whitecliff Rigg and Hawdale Rigg.

Moor names

The Moor, Dalby
Watmoor, Waltermoor or Watermoor. Possibly water or OE personal name Watt.
Pexton Moor is across the valley.

Stream names

Staindale, Dalby, Ellerburn and Thornton becks.

Meadow names

Haygate, Highgate, Low and other Ings.

House names

Coatehouse – from sheepcote: Keldhousegarth from spring house, Flaxdale End House and Sibdale End House.

Road names

Haygate and Highgate, Liddygate from ON hlid-slope and stie a path running uphill.
Swinegate – road for pigs.
Stannygate from OE stanig meaning stony or made of stone.
Risesty – from OE hris meaning rush and stie meaning uphill path.
Flaxdale Wath and Brayworth refer to fords.

Close names

Bouchard or Dutton   from personal names
Upper and lower fallows
Long crooks
Far close
Hill before the door
Calve close
Gross close
Sibdale End
Cleufield Rigg End
Hareborough Rigg End
Keldale End closes
Swardale close
Hollow
Hemp garth
Summer
Summer bottom
Paddock
East garth
North garth
Tup close   for rams
Low and upper longland   suggests mediaeval ploughing
Intake or summer cow pasture

Wood names

Dalby Haggs
Lower Hagg
Spring Hagg
Risestie or Haygate Hagg
Low Spring Hagg
Littlegate Hagg
Upper Hagg

APPENDIX 5

Forest verses

Oath of the Inhabitants of the Forest, being of the age of 12 years, used anciently in these old rhymes (supplied by the late Miss Grace Fox of Pickering).

> You shall true liege man be,
> Unto the King's majestie;
> Unto the beasts of the Forest you shall no hurt do
> Nor to any thing that doth belong thereunto.
> The offences of others you shall not conceal
> But, to the utmost of your power, you shall them reveal.
> Unto the Officers of the Forest,
> Or to them who may see them redrest,
> All these things you shall see done,
> So help you God, at His Holy Doom.

Old verse

In Forest Law, for venison offences all were principals, including anyone who received deer from another. According to this verse, you could plead that you didn't know what you were eating. It advises on good visiting manners.

> "It is not to be inquired from whence venison cometh,
>> For if by chance it stolen be,
>> A good belief sufficeth thee".

APPENDIX 6

Statute against hunting by landless people

Statutes of the Realm II.65

Also pray the commons that whereas artificers and labourers, that is to say, butchers, shoemakers, tailors, and other low persons, keep greyhounds and other dogs, and at times when good Christians on holy days are at church, hearing divine service, go hunting in parks, rabbit-runs and warrens of lords and others, and destroy them entirely; and so they assemble at such times to hold discussions, and make plots and conspiracies, to make insurrections and disobedience to your majesty and laws, under colour of such manner of hunting.

May it please you to ordain in this present Parliament, that any kind of artificer or labourer or any other who lacks lands and tenements to the value of 40s a year, or any priest or clerk if he has not preferment worth £10, shall not keep any greyhound, or any other dogs, if they are not fastened up or leashed, or have had their claws cut, on pain of imprisonment for a year. And that every justice of the peace shall have power to enquire and punish every contravention.

Reply: the King consents, adding to this, hounds and ferrets, hays, nets, hairpipes, cords and all other devices to take or destroy beasts of the forest, hares or rabbits, or other sport of gentlefolk.

APPENDIX 7

Deposition of Sir Robert Sawdane, priest, servant to Sir Roger Hastynges

"On Christynmas Day last past he was in his parish Church at Ellerburn, where he is vicar, and there, when he came to the Church and found Rauff Joynor there, and insomuch as he knewe that his maister luffyd not hym. Therefore he went to mete his said maister by the way and prayed hym that he wold in goddes peace ayeinst the said Rauff be, and thereupon he answered hym ageyn that Rauff Joynor and he would not be in oone Churche to gidre, and than the said deponent knelyng on his knees desired his said maister to suffre the said Rauff Joynor to be his in his parysshe church, insomuch as it was a solempne and a high day. And he said as he did before. And that if he taried in the Church it shuld be at his Jepardy, and thereupon or ever the said Sir Roger Hastinges had commanded hym to depart thens for Jeopardi of his liff".

APPENDIX 8

Records of the Eyre

Fines received at Pickering on Monday 2 December 1336, before Richard de Wylughby and John de Hambury. (Extract)

David de Neuton and Thomas de Neuton foresters, for a hart's hide, 1s 6d, and for concealing it 2s; bail Ralph de Morton.

For several offences in the forest, Thomas le Fletchere, servant of Richard de Helmesley 2s bail Ralph son of Matilda and Ralph de Morton; Ralph son of Matilda, late servant of Geoffrey de Kynthorp 3s 4d, and same bail.

Edmund de Hastyng, forester of Parnell de Kingthorp 3s, for 6 pigs in Dalby Laund, bail Thomas Bret.

John de Harlai, sworn forester in Langdale for 3 years, 3s 4d, for collecting sheaves and wool in the country under colour of his office and for keeping his servants at the cost of residents within the forest when he ought not, bail Ralph de Morton.

Thomas de Wyvelle for poaching 13s 4d, bail John de Pickering and Robert his brother. Richard son of Richard de Dalby, for taking pledges, though not sworn 2s; bail Richard de Dalby who pays the money into court.

Fines for harehunting, William son of Edmund de Hastynges 2s. Hugh de Neville 13s 4d; bail for each William de Creppyng.

John de Boyes, servant of the Dean of York for poaching, by taking with his hound a weak sore 6s 8d, bail Roger Trutcok, John de Malton, Henry Kelk and Ralph de Morton.

William de Towthorp of Ebberston for taking 2 cartloads of wood in Stayndale 1s, without livery of the foresters.

Agistments. John le Serjant agister of the west ward 6d for the year 1335.

Robert Serjant, woodward, 2s for taking money from every cart carrying livery wood from the forest.

APPENDIX 9

Booke of Olde Customs of Gawine Bebbington, 1632

The cattle brand for Dalby agistment

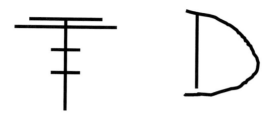

APPENDIX 10

Letter about poaching

Letter from William Wilmott, Steward to Mr John Hill 10th February 1746/7 (extract).

"Honourable Sir

I cannot say that I ever see many persons hunt of course, publickly, except Mr Hunter or some of the family, who frequently are a coursing, but altho they (the rest of the freeholders) do not hunt publickly, I may say that several of them do either hunt rabbits on the common in the night or set snares for them, or hares. Young Mr Warren has told me several times that he or some of the neighbours have at diverse times found many snares set in Buffet hedge. I have been credibly informed that James Boyes, or his son, has a lurching kind of a dog and always kept up in the house except at nights. I have seen the dog by chance in the day and he seems likely for that purpose. I also hear John Pickering the Quaker has a dog kept up in the same manner.

Yours honours most dutiful servant. Thornton".

APPENDIX 11

The Thornton and Farmanby Estate Survey of 1777

A Survey in 1777 listed lands within Dalby as

		A.r.p*				A.r.p	
673	Mrs Hill	4.0.12	Keldhouse Garth	685	Crown lease	12.0.5	Long Lands
674	Crown lease	6.0.2	Dalby Low Wood Close	686	" "	20.2.36	
675	" "	38.3.0	Low Wood	687	" "	5.0.32	
676	" "	14.0.12	Great Ings	688	" "	2.2.16	
677	" "	6.1.36	Little Ings	689	" "	9.1.2	High Wood
678	" "	6.3.0	" "	690	" "	24.1.28	" "
679	" "	15.1.16	Haygate Ings	691	" "	4.3.3	
680	" "	14.3.0	High Ings	692	" "	2.3.0	
681	" "	44.2.4	Haygate Wood	693	" "	1.3.8	
682	" "	24.3.0	High Wood	694	" "	4.1.4	
		1.2.6	Croft	695	" "	972.3.18	High Dalby Warren
683	" "	2.1.0	Tup Paddock	696	" "	792.0.24	Low Dalby Warren
684	" "	23.0.3					
Neighbouring land of interest included							
666	Dean of Windsor	29.3.4	Ellerburn Warren	697	Richard Hill	304.1.10	Flansey
667	"	47.3.6	"	698	" "	68.2.7	Flansey, not fenced from Thornton Common
668	"	24.1.5	"	699	Thornton freeholders	842.0.35	Thornton Common
672	"	75.1.16	"	700	Farmanby freeholders	675.3.30	Farmanby Common

* Acres, roods and perches

APPENDIX 12

Land use in Dalby Forest (Hectares)

		1976	2007
Dalby	Plantations	3404	3252 [1]
	Plantable	100	0 [2]
	Recreation		182 [3]
	Agricultural etc	1209	163 [4]
	TOTAL	4533	3597

Notes on 2007 figures added by B. Walker
1. This figure includes plantations at all stages of growth including; felled areas where the intention is to replant, research plantations, christmas tree stands and forest roads and rides. It is less than the 1976 figure due to enforced land sales in the late 1980's and early 1990's.
2. In 2007 no farm or other land in Dalby was regarded as a 'plantable reserve'.
3. The figure for recreation includes; unforested conservation areas, scheduled monuments and cultural heritage, old quarries and open water.
4. The low figure for 2007 is due to the enforced sale of agricultural land on the forest margins, particularly on Pexton Moor and at Bickley

APPENDIX 13

Forestry Commission Chief Foresters of Dalby Forest

Tom Anderson
Leonard Snowden   28 years
Tom Johnson   5 years
Arthur Bowns
Geoff Haw

A retired Forestry Commission worker recalls Tom Anderson as being the the first forester to have mechanised transport - a motor cycle and sidecar – and that Low Dalby House was barely habitable, Mr Anderson having to move his child's bed to avoid the incoming snow. After the retirement of Geoff Haw the management structure of local forests, including Dalby, changed and there ceased to be a single forester in charge of the forest.

APPENDIX 14

Estimates of growing stock, Pickering Forest District 1974

Pines   52%
Larches   16%
Hardwoods   4%   (Mainly Beech)
Spruces   22%
Other conifers   6%   (Mainly Douglas Fir)